CONGRESSIONAL POLICIES, PRACTICES AND PROCEDURES

EXPIRING FEDERAL TAX PROVISIONS

2012-2022

Congressional Policies, Practices and Procedures

Additional books in this series can be found on Nova's website under the Series tab.

Additional E-books in this series can be found on Nova's website under the E-book tab.

American Political, Economic, and Security Issues

Additional books in this series can be found on Nova's website under the Series tab.

Additional E-books in this series can be found on Nova's website under the E-book tab.

CONGRESSIONAL POLICIES, PRACTICES AND PROCEDURES

EXPIRING FEDERAL TAX PROVISIONS

2012-2022

PAUL L. COLLINS
AND
FRANK R. PETERSON
EDITORS

Nova Science Publishers, Inc.
New York

For permission to use material from this book please contact us:
Telephone 631-231-7269; Fax 631-231-8175
Web Site: http://www.novapublishers.com

Library of Congress Cataloging-in-Publication Data

ISBN: 978-1-62257-123-9

Published by Nova Science Publishers, Inc. † New York

CONTENTS

PREFACE

A number of tax provisions have either expired in 2011 or are scheduled to expire at the end of this FY 2012. These include the Bush tax cuts, the alternative minimum tax (AMT) patch, the temporary payroll tax cut, and other temporary expiring provisions, many of which are commonly referred to as "tax extenders." Aside from the payroll tax cut, which was extended by the Middle Class Tax Relief and Job Creation Act of 2012, the most recent law extending many of these provisions was the Tax Relief, Unemployment Insurance Reauthorization and Job Creation Act of 2010. This book provides an overview of these expiring provisions with a focus on past cost and cost of extension and a brief discussion of the current debate concerning the policy.

Chapter 1 - A number of tax provisions either expired in 2011 or are scheduled to expire at the end of this 2012. These include the following:

- The Bush tax cuts, which reduced income taxes by reducing tax rates, reducing the marriage penalty, repealing limitations on personal exemptions and itemized deductions (PEP and Pease, respectively), expanding refundable credits, and modifying education tax incentives. The Bush tax cuts also reduced estate tax liabilities by increasing the amount of an estate exempt from taxation and by lowering the tax rate.
- The alternative minimum tax (AMT) patch, which, by increasing the amount of income that is exempt from the AMT and allowing certain personal credits against the AMT, prevents an estimated 26 million additional taxpayers from owing the AMT.
- The payroll tax cut, which reduced an employee's share of Social Security taxes by two percentage points.

- A variety of previously extended temporary tax provisions, commonly referred to as "tax extenders," which affect individuals, businesses, charitable giving, energy, community development, and disaster relief.

As Congress decides whether to extend these provisions, it may consider the estimated revenue losses associated with their extension. The Congressional Budget Office (CBO) estimated that extending these provisions through 2022, except for the payroll tax cut, which CBO assumes expires as scheduled at the end of 2012, would reduce revenues by $5.4 trillion between 2013 and 2022. Specifically, over this 10-year budgetary window extending the Bush tax cuts and extending the AMT patch would reduce revenues by $4.6 trillion, while extending the tax extenders would reduce revenues by $839 billion. The cost of extending the payroll tax cut for one year (2012) was estimated to be $114 billion over the 2012-2022 budgetary window.

In addition to budgetary cost, Congress may also consider other factors when evaluating tax policy. For example, when considering extending the Bush tax cuts, policy makers might consider that the majority of the benefits of this policy accrued to the top 20% of taxpayers. They might also evaluate the potential contractionary impact the expiration of these cuts in 2013 may have on the economy, especially since both the scheduled expiration of the payroll tax cut and the enactment of budget cuts as part of the Budget Control Act (P.L. 112-25) are scheduled to go into effect at the same time. Similarly, Congress may examine the cost effectiveness of the payroll tax cut. According to CBO, the short-term stimulus impact of the payroll tax cut is lower than increasing aid to the unemployed or providing additional refundable tax credits to low- and middle-income households, but more stimulative than extending the Bush tax cuts. Finally, Congress may weigh the lower budgetary costs of short-term extensions of tax extenders against the unpredictability for taxpayers that can arise from short-term extensions.

In past years, Congress has extended expiring provisions en masse in one legislative vehicle. In the 112th Congress, Members have yet to consider legislation that would extend all of the provisions discussed in this report, although legislation to extend certain provisions has been considered.

Chapter 2 - This document,[1] prepared by the staff of the Joint Committee on Taxation, provides a listing of Federal tax provisions (other than those providing time-limited transition relief after the repeal of an underlying rule) that are currently scheduled to expire in 2011-2022 (with references to the applicable section of the Internal Revenue Code of 1986 or other applicable law).

In: Expiring Federal Tax Provisions: 2012-2022 ISBN: 978-1-62257-123-9
Editors: P. L. Collins and F. R. Peterson

Chapter 1

AN OVERVIEW OF TAX PROVISIONS EXPIRING IN 2012*

Margot L. Crandall-Hollick

SUMMARY

A number of tax provisions either expired in 2011 or are scheduled to expire at the end of this 2012. These include the following:

- The Bush tax cuts, which reduced income taxes by reducing tax rates, reducing the marriage penalty, repealing limitations on personal exemptions and itemized deductions (PEP and Pease, respectively), expanding refundable credits, and modifying education tax incentives. The Bush tax cuts also reduced estate tax liabilities by increasing the amount of an estate exempt from taxation and by lowering the tax rate.
- The alternative minimum tax (AMT) patch, which, by increasing the amount of income that is exempt from the AMT and allowing certain personal credits against the AMT, prevents an estimated 26 million additional taxpayers from owing the AMT.

---

* This is an edited, reformatted and augmented version of Congressional Research Service, Publication No. R42485, dated April 17, 2012.

- The payroll tax cut, which reduced an employee's share of Social Security taxes by two percentage points.
- A variety of previously extended temporary tax provisions, commonly referred to as "tax extenders," which affect individuals, businesses, charitable giving, energy, community development, and disaster relief.

As Congress decides whether to extend these provisions, it may consider the estimated revenue losses associated with their extension. The Congressional Budget Office (CBO) estimated that extending these provisions through 2022, except for the payroll tax cut, which CBO assumes expires as scheduled at the end of 2012, would reduce revenues by $5.4 trillion between 2013 and 2022. Specifically, over this 10-year budgetary window extending the Bush tax cuts and extending the AMT patch would reduce revenues by $4.6 trillion, while extending the tax extenders would reduce revenues by $839 billion. The cost of extending the payroll tax cut for one year (2012) was estimated to be $114 billion over the 2012-2022 budgetary window.

In addition to budgetary cost, Congress may also consider other factors when evaluating tax policy. For example, when considering extending the Bush tax cuts, policy makers might consider that the majority of the benefits of this policy accrued to the top 20% of taxpayers. They might also evaluate the potential contractionary impact the expiration of these cuts in 2013 may have on the economy, especially since both the scheduled expiration of the payroll tax cut and the enactment of budget cuts as part of the Budget Control Act (P.L. 112-25) are scheduled to go into effect at the same time. Similarly, Congress may examine the cost effectiveness of the payroll tax cut. According to CBO, the short-term stimulus impact of the payroll tax cut is lower than increasing aid to the unemployed or providing additional refundable tax credits to low- and middle-income households, but more stimulative than extending the Bush tax cuts. Finally, Congress may weigh the lower budgetary costs of short-term extensions of tax extenders against the unpredictability for taxpayers that can arise from short-term extensions.

In past years, Congress has extended expiring provisions en masse in one legislative vehicle. In the 112th Congress, Members have yet to consider legislation that would extend all of the provisions discussed in this report, although legislation to extend certain provisions has been considered.

INTRODUCTION

A number of tax provisions have either expired at the end of 2011 or are scheduled to expire at the end of this year.[1] These include the Bush tax cuts, the alternative minimum tax (AMT) patch, the temporary payroll tax cut, and other temporary expiring provisions, many of which are commonly referred to as "tax extenders." Aside from the payroll tax cut, which was extended by the Middle Class Tax Relief and Job Creation Act of 2012 (P.L. 112-96), the most recent law extending many of these provisions was the Tax Relief, Unemployment Insurance Reauthorization and Job Creation Act of 2010 (P.L. 111-312).

This report provides an overview of these expiring provisions. For each provision (or group of provisions), this report first describes the provision ("current law"), then outlines its past cost and if available the cost of its extension ("budgetary cost"), and concludes with a brief discussion of the current debate concerning the policy ("policy debate"). In the case of the Bush tax cuts and tax extenders, where the policies comprise a variety of other provisions, the details of the provisions are provided in accompanying tables.

In past years, Congress has extended expiring provisions en masse in one legislative vehicle.[2] In the 112th Congress, Members have yet to consider legislation that would extend all of the provisions discussed in this report past their scheduled expiration, although legislation to extend certain provisions has been considered.[3]

BUSH TAX CUTS

Current Law

The Bush tax cuts were provisions—enacted into law primarily by the Economic Growth and Tax Relief Reconciliation Act of 2001 (EGTRRA; P.L. 107-16) and the Jobs Growth Tax Relief Reconciliation Act of 2003 (JGTRRA; P.L. 108-27)—which gradually reduced individual income and estate tax liabilities between 2002 and 2010.[4,5] These tax cuts were extended for 2011 and 2012 by the Tax Relief, Unemployment Insurance Reauthorization, and Job Creation Act of 2010 (P.L. 111-312), henceforth referred to as the 2010 Tax Act. Notably, the 2010 Tax Act was enacted under President Obama, not President Bush, although the underlying policy is still commonly referred to as the Bush tax cuts.

A Comparison of 2012 Income Tax Brackets
Married Filing Jointly

Taxable Income	Bush Tax Cuts In Place (tax rate)	Bush Tax Cuts Expired (tax rate)
$0 - $17,400	10%	15%
$17,400 - $59,000	15%	15%
$59,000 - $70,700	15%	28%
$70,700 - $142,700	25%	28%
$142,700 - $217,450	28%	31%
$217,450 - $240,800	33%	36%
$240,800 - $388,350	33%	36%
$388,350 -	35%	39.6%
standard deduction	$11,900	$9,950
personal exemption	$3,800	$3,800

Source: Tax Policy Center and the Internal Revenue Service.

The Bush tax cuts lowered income taxes in a variety of ways (detailed in **Table 1**), including by

- reducing tax rates (see the shaded text box with a comparison of 2012 tax brackets under current law versus if the Bush tax cuts had hypothetically expired in 2012);[6]
- reducing long-term capital gains rates and the tax rate on dividends;
- reducing and then repealing income limitations for personal exemptions and itemized deductions (often referred to as PEP and Pease, respectively);[7]
- expanding tax credits, including the earned income tax credit (EITC), the child tax credit, the adoption tax credit, and the dependent care tax credit;
- reducing the marriage penalty; and
- modifying education tax incentives, including Coverdell education saving accounts (ESAs), the student loan interest deduction, and the tax treatment of certain scholarships and fellowships. The Bush tax cuts also created an exclusion for employer-provided educational assistance.

The Bush tax cuts also gradually reduced the estate tax[8] between 2002 and 2009, with a full repeal of the estate tax in 2010. Under EGTRRA, the amount of an estate which was exempt from taxation gradually rose from $1 million per decedent in 2002 to $3.5 million per decedent[9] in 2009, while the top tax rate under the estate tax fell from 50% to 45% over the same time period. In 2010, for the first time since 1916, there was no federal estate tax. The 2010 Tax Act reinstated the estate tax, but raised the exemption level and lowered the tax rate in comparison to the estate tax in effect in 2009. Specifically, the exemption amount in 2011 was set at $5 million per decedent (adjusted for inflation, this amount will equal $5,120,000 per decedent in 2012) and the top tax rate was set at 35%. The estate tax is scheduled to increase in 2013, with a $1 million per decedent exemption level and 55% top tax rate. Finally, the American Recovery and Reinvestment Act of 2009 (ARRA; P.L. 111-5) made modifications to two provisions of the Bush tax cuts and enacted two new tax provisions. Specifically, ARRA's modifications expanded the refundability of the child tax credit and further reduced the marriage penalty of the EITC (described in **Table 1**). These changes were extended along with the Bush tax cuts by the 2010 Tax Act. In addition, ARRA increased the EITC for families with three or more children[10] and enacted a new higher education tax credit—the American Opportunity Tax Credit (AOTC).[11] These tax law changes were also extended through the end of 2012 by the 2010 Tax Act.

Budgetary Cost

The 2010 Tax Act's two-year extension of the income and estate tax provisions of the Bush tax cuts (including the four ARRA modifications) reduced revenues by $475.79 billion over a 10-year budgetary window (2011-2020).[12] Of these revenue losses, $363.55 billion is attributable to the extension of the income tax provisions of EGTRRA and JGTRRA, $68.15 billion is attributable to the modified estate tax provision, and $44.10 billion is attributable to the four ARRA tax provisions discussed above.[13] The Congressional Budget Office (CBO) estimated that the extension of the income and estate tax provisions[14] of the Bush tax cuts and the four ARRA tax provisions through 2022 would cost $2.84 trillion over a 10-year budgetary window (2013 2022).[15] The debt service associated with extending these provisions was estimated to be $505 billion over the same time period.

Policy Debate

Supporters and opponents of the Bush tax cuts generally evaluate the Bush tax cuts from different perspectives. Supporters of the tax cuts stress their long-term and short-term economic benefits. Opponents often emphasize that the tax cuts are costly in terms of reduced revenues and that the benefits of this policy disproportionally accrue to the highest income taxpayers.

When the Bush tax cuts were originally proposed, proponents stressed that by reducing marginal tax rates, this policy would lessen some of the distortions taxes had on work, saving, and investment, ultimately boosting long-term growth. For example, by reducing marginal tax rates, individuals would have more take-home pay, theoretically incentivizing them to work more.

Ultimately, this increased economic activity would boost long-term economic growth. Some critics have sought to disprove this theory by comparing historical growth rates and marginal tax rates in the United States. They argue that in periods when taxes where raised (the mid to late 1990s for example), growth was higher than in periods when taxes were cut (the 2000s for example).

However, comparing growth rates during periods with different tax rates does not necessarily prove that tax policy *did not* impact growth since a variety of other factors, aside from tax rates, differ between these time periods. The results of many economic studies, have shown that tax cuts generally do affect growth (and components of growth).[16] They have also generally shown, however, that the impact of tax cuts on growth is small in relation to the foregone revenue resulting from the cut.[17]

When the Bush tax cuts were being considered by Congress in 2001, the economy had slipped into a recession.

Tax-cut advocates were highlighting the short-term stimulative benefits of the tax cuts. Estimates prepared at the time the Bush tax cuts were being considered predicted a short-term stimulative effect.[18]

In addition, CBO analysis indicated that reductions in individual income tax rates could have short-term stimulative impacts on the economy, although these effects were estimated to be small.[19]

Later analysis concluded that "the tax cuts reduced GDP [gross domestic product] and employment in 2001, and had virtually no effect on those aggregates in 2002."[20] More recent estimates by CBO concluded that the tax cuts had limited stimulative benefit—estimating that every $1 dollar of Bush tax cuts resulted in 10 to 60 cents of GDP.[21]

Yet, while the Bush tax cuts may not have been an effective short-term stimulus *in response to a recession*, some economists warn that allowing these tax cuts to expire in 2013, at the same time as a scheduled fiscal contraction, may have a negative effect on the economy.[22]

Opponents of the Bush tax cuts highlight both their high cost as well as the fact that most of the benefits go to upper-income taxpayers. Recent estimates by CBO indicate that the Bush tax cuts, whose cost were not offset, increased the deficit by $1.75 trillion over the past 10 years (2002- 2011).[23] Estimates indicate that approximately two-thirds of the benefits of these cuts accrued to the top 20% of taxpayers with the highest income[24] and over one quarter (26.5%) of the benefits of the Bush tax cuts accrued to the top 1%.[25] By contrast less than a fifth of the benefits (16.5%) accrued to the bottom 60% of taxpayers.[26] Critics charge that this distribution of benefits is "unfair." In response, supporters of the tax cuts approach the "fairness" of the tax cuts from a different perspective. They highlight that higher income taxpayers pay a greater share of federal taxes, and the tax cut was fair in so far as it benefitted the taxpayers with the highest tax burdens. According to CBO, the top 20% of households in the income distribution pay more than two-thirds (68.9%) of all federal tax liabilities, while the top 1% of households pays more than a quarter of all Federal taxes (28.1%).[27]

Another perspective on the "fairness" of these tax cuts that opponents of this policy highlight is their distributional impact on after-tax income. According to estimates examining tax burdens in 2010, the Bush tax cuts resulted in the lowest 20% of taxpayers seeing their income rise by 0.5%, while the top 20% saw their after-tax incomes rise by 4.9% and the top 1% saw their income rise by 6.6%.[28]

The distributional impact of the Bush tax cuts may be relevant to policy makers if they are concerned with growing income inequality in the United States.[29] A recent CBO report highlighted that while the main driver of increasing after-tax income inequality was the increasing concentration of *pre-tax income* among the wealthiest Americans, government transfers and federal tax policy also contributed to the growth of after-tax income inequality.[30] As the CBO report indicated, the equalizing impact of taxes depends on their progressivity,[31] with increasing progressivity reducing income inequality (holding the size of tax receipts constant).[32] The Bush tax cuts overall reduced the progressivity of federal income taxes[33] and hence were a factor in increases in income inequality in the United States. When evaluated separately, some Bush tax cut provisions increased income inequality, while others contributed to a decrease in income inequality. Recent CRS analysis found that the lowering of tax rates, the repeal of PEP and Pease, and the reduced taxes on capital gains and dividends increased income inequality. Alternatively, the expansion of the child tax credit and EITC were found to reduce income inequality.[34]

Table 1. Major Provisions of the Bush Tax Cuts

Provision	Bush Tax Cuts In Effect (2011-2012)	Bush Tax Cuts Expired (Post-2012)
Tax Rates and Brackets		
10% Tax Bracket	This tax bracket applies to the first $7,000 of taxable income for single filers / $14,000 of taxable income for married joint filers. Income thresholds for this bracket are adjusted annually for inflation and equal $8,700 and $17,400, respectively for the 2012 tax year.	This bracket expires and taxable income that was previously subject to the 10% rate will be subject to the 15% rate.
Tax Rates in Top Four Tax Brackets	35% | 33% | 28% | 25%	39.6% | 36% | 31% | 28%
Tax Rates on Capital Gains and Dividends	The top tax rate for both long-term capital gains and dividends is 15%.	The top rate for long-term capital gains will rise to 20% and dividends will be taxed at ordinary income tax rates.
Limits on Personal Exemptions and Itemized Deductions		
Limits on Itemized Deductions (Pease)	There are no income limits on the overall amount of itemized deductions a taxpayer can claim.	The limit on itemized deductions will be restored. For higher income taxpayers, the total amount of itemized deductions will be reduced by 3% of the amount by which the taxpayer's AGI exceeds an applicable threshold, adjusted annually for inflation. The total amount of itemized deductions will not be reduced by more than 80%. (In 2011, the applicable threshold if Pease had been in effect would have been $169,550).
Personal Exemptions Phase-Out (PEP)	There are no income restrictions on the amount of personal exemptions a taxpayer can claim.	The limit on personal exemptions will be restored. For higher income taxpayers, the total amount of exemptions that can be claimed will be reduced by 2% for each $2,500 by which the taxpayer's AGI exceeds applicable thresholds, adjusted annually for inflation. In 2011, the applicable thresholds if PEP was in effect would have been $169,500 for single filers and $254,350 for married joint filers.

Provision	Bush Tax Cuts In Effect (2011-2012)	Bush Tax Cuts Expired (Post-2012)
Children and Familiesa		
Child Tax Credit	The child credit is $1,000 per eligible child. The child tax credit is partially refundable using the earned income formula which is equal to 15% of a family's earnings in excess of a refundability threshold of $10,000 (indexed for inflation annually). ARRA lowered the refundability threshold used in the formula to $3,000 (not indexed for inflation) for 2009 and 2010.b This lower threshold was extended for 2011 and 2012 by P.L. 111-312.	The child credit will be $500 per eligible child. The child tax credit will be non-refundable for most families (the earned income formula expires).
Adoption Tax Benefitsc	Eligible taxpayers can claim two adoption tax benefits, although the combined level of qualified expenses was limited to $13,360 in 2011. Specifically, a taxpayer could either exclude from their income up to $13,360 of employer provided adoption assistance in 2011 or claim a tax credit of up to $13,360, or a combination of both tax benefits as long as the combined level of qualified expenses does not exceed $13,360. In 2012, the combined limit for qualified expenses is $12,650. Both the tax credit and exclusion phase-out for taxpayers with incomes between $185,210-$225,210 in 2011 and $189,710-$229,710 in 2012.	The adoption tax credit will be available only for special needs adoptions. The exclusion for employer provided adoption assistance will expire. The limit for the credit will be reduced to $6,000 (not indexed for inflation). The phase-out range for the credit will be $75,000-$115,000 (not indexed for inflation).
Dependent Care Tax Credit	The dependent care credit is equal to 35% of the first $3,000 of eligible expenses for one qualifying individual ($6,000 of qualifying expenses for two or more eligible individuals). The 35% credit rate is reduced for incomes above $15,000.	The dependent care credit will be equal to 30% of the first $2,400 of eligible expenses for one qualifying individual ($4,800 for two or more qualifying individuals). The 30% credit rate will be reduced for incomes above $10,000.
Marriage Penalty		
Standard Deduction for Married Couples	The deduction for married couples is 200% the deduction for singles	The deduction for married couples will be 167% the deduction for singles.
15% Bracket for Married Couples	The upper limit of this bracket is equal to 200% (i.e. double) the upper limit for singles.	The upper limit of this bracket will be equal to 167% of the upper limit for singles.

Table 1. (Continued)

Provision	Bush Tax Cuts In Effect (2011-2012)	Bush Tax Cuts Expired (Post-2012)
Earned Income Tax Credit	The income level at which the EITC begins to phase-out was increased by $3,000 under EGTRRA. This amount was increased to $5,000 by ARRA (this amount was indexed for inflation after 2008). Hence, in 2012 the EITC phase-out range for an unmarried taxpayer with two children is $17,090-$41,952, while the phase-out range for a married taxpayer with two children is $22,300-$47,162 (a difference of $5,210).	The higher phase-out level for married taxpayers will expire and their phase-out levels will be the same as for unmarried taxpayers.
Education Benefitsd		
Employer Provided Educational Assistance	Up to $5,250 of qualifying employer provided educational assistance is excluded from income and hence not subject to taxation.	Provision expires.e
Student Loan Interest Deduction	Up to $2,500 of student loan interest expenses can be deducted from gross income (as an above-the-line deduction). The amount that can be deducted phases out between $60,000-$75,000 for single filers and $120,000-$150,000 for married joint filers for 2011. For 2012, the phase-out level for married joint filers rises to $125,000-$155,000 and remains the same for single filers.	The deduction can only be claimed by eligible taxpayers for the first 60 months (5 years) of interest payments. In addition, the income phase-out levels are reduced to $40,000-$55,000 for single filers and $60,000-$75,000 for married joint filers, adjusted for inflation occurring since 2002.
Coverdells Education Savings Accounts (ESAs)	Coverdell ESAs are modified in several ways, including: (1) The maximum contribution amount for a beneficiary is $2,000 per year (2) Qualified expenses include elementary and secondary school expenses (kindergarten through 12th grade), in addition to higher education expenses (3) The phase-out range for married taxpayers is $190,000-$220,000 (double the phase-out range for singles) (4) Age limitations are waived for special needs beneficiaries (5) Beneficiaries who use Coverdells, can also claim education tax credits without penalty (expenses paid for with Coverdell funds cannot be used to claim credits)	These modifications expire, hence: (1) The maximum contribution amount for a beneficiary will be $500 per year (2) Qualified expenses will be limited to higher education expenses (3) The phase-out range for married taxpayers will be $150,000-$160,000 (4) Contributions can be made up until the beneficiary is 18 years old and all distributions must be made when the beneficiary turns 30 for both non-special needs and special needs beneficiaries

Provision	Bush Tax Cuts In Effect (2011-2012)	Bush Tax Cuts Expired (Post-2012)
	(6) Contribution can be made to both a 529 and Coverdell for the same beneficiary without penalty	(5) If taxpayers claim education tax credits when they take a Coverdell distribution, their distribution will be subject to taxation (6) Contributions made to a Coverdell for a beneficiary will be subject to a 6% excise tax if contributions for the same beneficiary are made to a 529 in the same year
Tax Treatment of National Health Service Corps Scholarships and F. Edward Herbert Armed Forces Health Professions Scholarship and Financial Assistance Programs	Students must generally pay taxes on any part of a scholarship, fellowship, or tuition reduction that can be attributed to teaching, research, or other services that have been performed, are being performed, or will be performed. A temporary exception to this general rule is allowed for funding received from the National Health Service Corps Scholarship Program and the F. Edward Hebert Armed Forces Health Professions Scholarship and Financial Assistance Program.	Funding received from the National Health Service Corps Scholarship Program and the F. Edward Hebert Armed Forces Health Professions Scholarship and Financial Assistance Program will be included as part of income and hence subject to taxation.
Estate Tax		
Exemption Level and Top Rate	Gradually, the top exemption amount increased and the top tax rate decreased from $1million per decedent / 50% in 2002 to $3.5 million per decedent / 45% in 2009. There was no estate tax in 2010. P.L. 111-312 modified the estate tax for 2011 and 2012. The exemption amount is equal to $5 million per decedent indexed for inflation and the top tax rate was 35%. In 2012, the basic exemption amount equals $5,120,000.	The top exemption amount will fall to $1 million per decedent (not indexed for inflation) and the top tax rate will rise to 55%.

Source: Joint Committee on Taxation, Summary of Provisions Contained in the Conference Agreement for H.R. 1836, the Economic Growth and Tax Relief Reconciliation Act of 2001, May 26, 2001, JCX-50-01, Joint Committee on Taxation, Technical Explanation of the Revenue Provisions Contained in the 'Tax Relief, Unemployment Insurance Reauthorization, and Job Creation Act of 2010' Scheduled for Consideration by the United States Senate, 111th Cong., December 10, 2010, JCX-55-10 and CRS Report R41111, Expiration and Extension of the Individual Income Tax Cuts First Enacted in 2001 and 2003: Background and Analysis, by James M. Bickley and the Internal Revenue Service, http://www.irs.gov/pub/irs-drop/rp-11-52.pdf.

a EGTRRA also included an employer-provided child care credit for businesses taxpayers and allowed Alaska Native Settlement Trusts to tax income to the trust, not the beneficiaries. These provisions, which were originally scheduled to expire at the end of 2010, were extended through the end of 2012 by P.L. 111-312.

b The Emergency Economic Stabilization Act (EESA; P.L. 110-343) lowered the refundability threshold to $8,500 for 2008.

c EGTRRA increased the dollar limitation on the credit and the exclusion for employer-provided adoption assistance to $10,000 (indexed to inflation after 2002) for all adoptions and increased the income phase-out starting point to $150,000 (indexed for inflation after 2002). Both of these modifications were set to expire at the end of 2010. The Patient Protection and Affordable Care Act (P.L. 111-148) increased the maximum amount of the credit to $13,170 for tax year 2010, with this amount indexed for inflation for 2011, and made the adoption credit refundable for 2010 and 2011. For more information, see CRS Report RL33633, *Tax Benefits for Families: Adoption*, by Christine Scott.

d EGTRRA also increased the arbitrage rebate exception from $10 million to $15 million for government bonds used to finance qualified school construction and allowed for the issuance of tax exempt private activity bonds for qualified education facilities.

e In the absence of this provision, taxpayers may still be able to exclude certain employer-provided educational assistance. Specifically, taxpayers can exclude employer-provided education assistance if it qualifies as a working condition fringe benefit. Generally, education expenses are qualify as a working condition fringe benefit if they would have been deductible under section 162 of the internal revenue code (IRC) and the employer paid them. According to section 162, qualifying education expenses are those associated with education that (1) maintains or improves a skill required in a trade or business of the taxpayer or (2) meets the requirements of taxpayer's employer, applicable law or regulation imposed as a condition of continued employment.

AMT PATCH

Current Law

The Alternative Minimum Tax (AMT) was designed to ensure that higher-income taxpayers who owed little or no taxes under the regular income tax because they could claim tax preferences would still pay some tax.[35] When calculating the AMT, taxpayers first add back various "tax preference items" (like certain deductions) to their taxable income, to determine the amount of income subject to the AMT (the "AMT tax base"). Second, taxpayers subtract a basic exemption amount from their AMT tax base. Third, a two-tiered rate structure of 26% and 28% is assessed against the AMT tax base to determine tax liability.

Finally, if a taxpayer's AMT is greater than their regular tax liability, the taxpayer pays the difference in addition to their regular tax liability (the difference paid is technically the AMT). Crucially, unlike the regular income tax, key parts of the AMT—including the exemption amounts—are not indexed for inflation. This means in a typical year, as a result of inflation increasing taxpayers' nominal income levels, additional taxpayers are subject to the AMT.

The Bush tax cuts temporarily increased the exemption amount under the AMT. This temporary increase in the exemption amount, known as the AMT patch, was extended several more times[36]—most recently by P.L. 111-312—and was in effect through the end of 2011.[37] In 2011, the AMT-exemption amounts were $74,450 for married individuals filing joint returns and $48,450 for unmarried individuals.

These exemption amounts revert to $45,000 for married individuals and $33,750 for unmarried individuals in 2012.[38] In addition, an AMT patch generally has also included a provision which allowed taxpayers to reduce their AMT by nonrefundable personal tax credits.[39] In 2012, under current law, most nonrefundable personal credits will no longer be allowed against the AMT.

Budgetary Cost

The JCT estimated that a one-year AMT patch for 2012 would reduce revenues by $92 billion over the 2012-2021 budgetary window.[40] The cost of longer-term AMT patches will depend on whether current tax policy (i.e., the Bush tax cuts) is also extended. Generally, for taxpayers subject to the AMT, the lower their taxes under the regular income tax system, the higher their AMT and, hence, the greater the cost to patch the AMT.

Thus, the cost of AMT patch would be expected to be higher if the Bush tax cuts—which generally lowered taxes—were in effect as compared to if they were not in effect, all else being equal. CBO estimates indicate that revenue losses from extending the AMT-patch concurrently with the Bush tax cuts are larger than only extending the AMT-patch and allowing the Bush tax cuts to expire.

The cost of indexing the AMT to inflation through 2022, assuming current law (i.e., the Bush tax cuts expire), is estimated to be $804 billion over 10 years, 2013-2022 (plus an additional $133 billion in debt service over the same time period).[41] CBO estimated that the combined cost of the extension of the Bush tax cuts and the AMT patch would be $920 billion more than the sum of extending these policies separately, highlighting the interaction between the regular income tax and AMT previously discussed.

Specifically, the cost of extending the Bush tax cuts was estimated to be $2.84 trillion over 10 years (2013-2022), while the cost of extending the AMT patch was estimated to be $804 billion over the same time period.

The cost of extending the policies concurrently was estimated to be $4.56 trillion between 2013 and 2022 (the debt service associated with a concurrent extension of the Bush tax cuts and the AMT patch was estimated to be an additional $790 billion between 2013 and 2022).[42]

Policy Debate

The current debate on the AMT patch centers around limiting the number of taxpayers subject to the AMT, while also minimizing the revenue losses to the federal government from the AMT patch. The AMT patch, if extended, would reduce the number of taxpayers subject to the AMT by approximately 26 million.[43] Many of these taxpayers are middle- and upper-middle income taxpayers—especially those with children. However, as previously discussed, the patch is costly in terms of lost revenue. Congress may choose to consider indexing the AMT for inflation or it may choose to reform the regular income tax system in such a way that the AMT no longer exists.[44]

PAYROLL TAX CUT

Current Law

The payroll tax cut—initially enacted for 2011 by P.L. 111-312 and extended for 2012 by P.L. 112-78 and P.L. 112-96—reduced the employee's share of Social Security payroll taxes.[45] Specifically, the payroll tax cut reduced the employee's share[46] of Social Security taxes from 6.2% to 4.2% for employees and from 12.4% to 10.4% for the self-employed on the first $110,100 of wages in 2012.[47]

Budgetary Cost

The total cost of the payroll tax cut for 2011 and 2012 has been estimated to be $225.7 billion for the 2011-2022 budgetary window.[48] Of this total cost, the 2011 payroll tax cut reduced revenues by $111.7 billion between 2011 and 2020, and the 2012 payroll tax cut reduced revenues by $114.0 billion between 2012 and 2022.[49]

Policy Debate

The payroll tax cut was intended to provide an economic stimulus by increasing workers' take-home pay. This tax cut benefits virtually all working Americans, but research indicates that this policy may not be as targeted or cost-effective a stimulus as other tax policies or direct-spending programs. Approximately 159 million workers will be eligible for the payroll tax cut in 2012, which on average will equal approximately $717 per worker.[50] However, the actual value will depend on the taxpayer's wages, with those making $20,000 receiving an additional $400 in take-home pay, and those making $110,100 or more (the Social Security wage cap in 2012) receiving a maximum increase of $2,202 in take-home pay.

Because the payroll tax cut is not targeted to those facing the greatest fiscal constraints (it is available to 94%[51] of wage earners irrespective of income level), a portion of it may be saved instead of spent, limiting the stimulative impact of this policy.[52] The Congressional Budget Office—which assumed that the majority of the increase in disposable income would be saved or used to pay down debt rather than spent on goods and services—estimated that a temporary reduction of payroll taxes would raise output cumulatively in the next two years by between 10 and 90 cents per dollar of total budgetary cost and would increase employment by between one and nine jobs per million dollars of budgetary cost.[53] According to CBO, the short-term stimulus impact of the payroll tax cut is lower than increasing aid to unemployed or providing additional refundable tax credits to low- and middle-income households (but on par with extending the AMT-patch). However, the same report indicated that the payroll tax cut was more stimulative in the short term than extending the Bush tax cuts. In addition, at the end of 2011 when the payroll tax cut was originally scheduled to expire, several economic reports indicated that its expiration could hamper economic growth.[54] Finally, policymakers may be concerned that this temporary provision could become a provision which is routinely extended. They may be concerned about the budgetary impact of these routine extensions. Or they may have concerns that routine extensions will negatively impact the Social Security trust fund, although the current payroll tax cut requires that the Social Security trust funds be "made whole" by a transfer of general revenue.

OTHER EXPIRING PROVISIONS AND "TAX EXTENDERS"

Current Law

In addition to temporary income, estate, AMT, and payroll tax provisions, Congress has enacted a variety of temporary tax provisions that either expired at the end of 2011 or are scheduled to expire at the end of 2012.[55] These provisions generally fall into one of six categories: those related to individuals, businesses, charitable giving, energy, community development, or disaster relief.

Table 2 provides a list of provisions that expired in 2011 or are scheduled to expire at the end of 2012, including information on the estimated 10-year cost of extending the provision for one year. Importantly, while most of the provisions that expired in 2011 or are scheduled to expire at the end of 2012 have been *routinely* extended on a short-term basis, and are hence commonly referred to as "tax extenders," there are a variety of expiring provisions that have not been previously extended. Both traditional "tax extenders" and these new expiring provisions are included in Table 2.

Individual

Several temporary tax provisions affecting individuals either expired at the end of 2011 or are scheduled to expire at the end of 2012. Of these, the largest in terms of estimated revenue losses include the deduction for state and local sales taxes;[56] the refundability of the credit for prior minimum tax liability; the above-the-line deduction for qualified tuition and related expenses;[57] the deduction of mortgage insurance premiums as qualified interest; the expansion of the adoption credit and adoption assistance programs;[58] the above-the-line deduction for certain expenses of elementary and secondary school teachers;[59] and the parity in the tax treatment of employer-provided transit benefits to parking benefits.

Business

Several temporary tax provisions affecting businesses either expired at the end of 2011 or are scheduled to expire at the end of 2012. Of these, the largest in terms of estimated revenue losses include bonus depreciation in 2011 and 2012, whereby a 100% bonus depreciation allowance is in effect through the end of 2011, set to decrease to 50% for 2012 and expire after December 31, 2012; the research and experimentation credit;[60] the exception under Subpart F for active financing income earned by banking, financing, and insurance business operations abroad;[61] the enhanced cost-recovery for qualified leasehold, restaurant, and retail improvements; and the enhanced expensing allowances which allow businesses to expense $500,000 for investment in qualified investment in 2011, $125,000 in 2012, and $25,000 thereafter.[62]

Charitable

Several temporary provisions designed to incentivize charitable giving[63] expired at the end of 2011. Of these, the largest in terms of estimated revenue losses include tax-free distributions from IRAs for the purposes of charitable donations; enhanced charitable deductions for corporate contributions of computer equipment for education purposes; and enhanced charitable deductions for contributions of food inventory.

Energy

Several temporary provisions affecting the energy sector, including alternative energy, expired at the end of 2011 or are scheduled to expire at the end of 2012. Of these, the largest in terms of estimated revenue losses include incentives for alcohol fuels (primarily ethanol); incentives for biodiesel and renewable diesel;[64] the Section 1603 grants-in-lieu of tax credit;[65] the placed-inservice date for the production tax credit for wind; and the credit for nonbusiness energy property (sometimes referred to as the "25C credit").[66]

Community Development

Several provisions to promote community development expired at the end of 2011. These include qualified zone academy bonds, which are available to state and local governments for elementary and secondary school renovation, equipment, teacher training, and course materials; the new markets tax credit (NMTC), which is designed to promote investment in low-income and impoverished communities;[67] and tax incentives to encourage economic activity in empowerment zones,[24] the District of Columbia (DC), and in the American Samoa.[68]

Disaster Relief Provisions

A number of disaster-related tax provisions expired at the end of 2011 or are scheduled to expire at the end of 2012. They include provisions designed to help redevelopment of the New York Liberty Zone and the Gulf Opportunity (GO) Zone,[69] as well as provisions to provide relief following the Midwestern storms and Hurricane Ike in 2008.

Budgetary Cost

The revenue losses from extending the tax extender provisions depends on which provisions are extended and the duration of the extension. The Joint Committee on Taxation (JCT) estimated that the cost of extending temporary provisions that expired in 2011 through the end of 2012 was $42.92 billion dollars over the 2012-2021 budgetary window.[70] The U.S. Treasury estimated that extending *certain* temporary provisions that expired in 2011 and 2012 through the end of 2013 was $26 billion over the 2013-2022 budgetary window.[71] CBO estimated that the revenue losses from extending temporary provisions[72] for a longer period than one or two years—through 2022—would reduce revenues by $839 billion over the 2013-2022 budgetary window.[73] The debt service associated with financing these extensions was estimated to be $173 billion over the same period.

Policy Debate

Congress may enact tax provisions on a temporary basis for a variety of reasons, including to provide short-term stimulus (e.g., the enhanced expensing provisions), to provide short-term disaster relief, or to encourage Congress to re-evaluate the efficacy of these provisions on a routine basis. The budgetary cost of a short-term extension is less than the cost of a longer-term extension, which some analysts contend is a major reason that these provisions are extended on a short-term basis.[74] At a recent Senate Finance Committee hearing on tax extenders, Dr. Roseanne Altshuler stated

> ...temporary tax legislation may simply (but sadly) be the result of Congress playing a budget game. The Congressional Budget Office (CBO) must project the revenue baseline using current law.

> This means that the CBO must assume that temporary provisions expire as scheduled. If, as past history would strongly suggest, temporary provisions are never allowed to lapse, then they effectively become permanent feature of the code that are not accounted for in the revenue baseline.
>
> Since almost all extenders involve tax cuts, the assumption they will be terminated tends to make the CBO project a healthier revenue baseline than is likely to occur.[75]

But while the temporary nature of these provisions and the resulting budgetary score may make them more politically palatable, some policymakers contend that the temporary nature of these provisions, and the uncertainty about whether they will be extended, limits their ability to achieve their policy objectives.[76]

CONCLUDING REMARKS

As Congress decides whether to extend some or all of these expiring tax provisions, it may consider several options. It may choose to extend all expiring tax provisions. CBO estimated that extending these provisions through 2022 (except for the payroll tax cut, which CBO assumes expires as scheduled at the end of 2012) would reduce revenues by $5.4 trillion between 2013 and 2022.

Specifically, over this 10-year budgetary window, extending the Bush tax cuts and extending the AMT patch would reduce revenues by $4.6 trillion, while extending other expiring provisions and "tax extenders" would reduce revenues by $839 billion.

The cost of extending the payroll tax cut for one year (2012) was estimated to be $114 billion over the 2012-2022 budgetary window. The extension of these provisions, if they are not offset, would increase the 10-year cumulative (2013-2022) deficit from $3.07 trillion to $9.44 trillion (including $963 billion in debt service between 2013 and 2022).

This would result in projected deficits as a percentage of GDP (a measure of deficits in proportion to the economy) rising from 1.5% to 4.7%, a figure many economists view as unsustainable.[77]

The deficit would be even higher if the payroll tax cut is extended again and is not offset.

Table 2. Temporary Tax Provisions and "Tax Extenders" Expiring in 2011 and 2012

Provision	Expiration Year	Internal Revenue Code Section	Most Recent Law Which Extended Provision	10-Year-Cost Estimate for 1-Year Extension (billions)
Individual Provisions				
Above-the-Line Deduction for Certain Expenses of Elementary and Secondary School Teachers	2011	Sec. 62(a)(2)(D)	P.L. 111-312	$0.23
Deduction for State and Local Sales Taxes	2011	Sec. 164(b)(5)	P.L. 111-312	$2.79
Above-the-Line Deduction for Qualified Tuition and Related Expenses	2011	Sec. 222(e)	P.L. 111-312	$0.78
Estate Tax Look-Through for Certain Regulated Investment Company (RIC) Stock Held by Nonresidents	2011	Sec. 2105(d)	P.L. 111-312	$0.01
Premiums for Mortgage Insurance Deductible as Qualified Interest	2011	Sec. 163(h)(3)	P.L. 111-312	$0.74
Parity for Exclusion for Employer-Provided Mass Transit and Parking Benefits	2011	Sec. 132(f)	P.L. 111-312	$0.16
Disclosure of Prisoner Return Information to Certain Prison Officials	2011	Sec. 6103(k)(10)	P.L. 110-428a	b
Treatment of Military Basic Housing Allowance under Low-Income Housing Credit	2011	Sec. 142(d)	P.L. 110-289a	c
Expansion of Adoption Credit and Adoption Assistance Programs	2011	Secs. 36C and 137; Sec. 10909(c) of P.L. 111-148	P.L. 111-148	d
Refunds Disregarded in the Administration of Federal Programs and Federally Assisted Programs	2012	Sec. 6409	P.L. 111-312a	e
Credit for Prior Year Minimum Tax Liability Made Refundable After Period of Years	2012	Sec. 53(e)	P.L. 109-432a	$0.93f
Business Provisions				
Tax Credit for Research and Experimentation Expenses	2011	Sec. 41(h)(1)(B)	P.L. 111-312	$7.65
Temporary Increase in Limit on Cover-Over of Rum Excise Tax Revenues to Puerto Rico and the Virgin Islands	2011	Sec. 7625(f)	P.L. 111-312	$0.13
Expensing of "Brownfield" Environmental Remediation Costs	2011	Sec. 198(h)	P.L. 111-312	$0.18

Provision	Expiration Year	Internal Revenue Code Section	Most Recent Law Which Extended Provision	10-Year-Cost Estimate for 1-Year Extension (billions)
Work Opportunity Tax Credit	2011	Sec. 51(c)(4)	P.L. 111-312	$0.97
Indian Employment Tax Credit	2011	Sec. 45A(f)	P.L. 111-312	$0.06
Accelerated Depreciation for Business Property on Indian Reservations	2011	Sec. 168(j)(8)	P.L. 111-312	$0.09
Exceptions under Subpart F for Active Financing Income	2011	Sec. 953(e)(1) and Sec. 954(h)(9)	P.L. 111-312	$5.21
Look-Through Treatment of Payments Between Controlled Foreign Corporations under the Foreign Personal Holding Company Rules	2011	Sec. 954(c)(6)	P.L. 111-312	$0.78
Credit for Railroad Track Maintenance	2011	Sec. 45G(f)	P.L. 111-312	$0.17
15-Year Straight-Line Cost Recovery for Qualified Leasehold, Restaurant, and Retail Improvements	2011	Secs. 168(e)(3)(E)(iv), (v), (ix); Secs.168(e)(7)(A)(i) and 168 (e)(8)	P.L. 111-312	$2.93
7-Year Recovery for Motorsport Racing Facilities	2011	Sec. 168(i)(15) and Sec. 168(e)(3)(C)(ii)	P.L. 111-312	$0.03
Deduction Allowable with Respect to Income Attributable to Domestic Production Activities in Puerto Rico	2011	Sec. 199(d)(8)	P.L. 111-312	$0.20
Modification of Tax Treatment of Certain Payments to Controlling Exempt Organizations	2011	Sec. 512(b)(13)(E)	P.L. 111-312	$0.02
Treatment of Certain Dividends of Regulated Investment Companies ("RICs")	2011	Secs. 871(k)(1)(C) and (2)(C); Secs. 881(e)(1)(A) and (2)	P.L. 111-312	$0.10
Employer Wage Credit for Activated Military Reservists	2011	Sec. 45P	P.L. 111-312	g
Special Expensing Rules for Film and Television Production	2011	Sec. 181(f)	P.L. 111-312	$0.12
RIC Qualified Investment Entity Treatment under FIRPTA	2011	Sec. 897(h)(4)	P.L. 111-312	$0.06
Special Rules for Qualified Small Business Stock	2011	Sec. 1202(a)(4)	P.L. 111-312	$1.21

Table 2. (Continued)

Provision	Expiration Year	Internal Revenue Code Section	Most Recent Law Which Extended Provision	10-Year-Cost Estimate for 1-Year Extension (billions)
Additional First-Year Depreciation for 100% of Basis of Qualified Property	2011	Sec. 168(k)(5)	P.L. 111-312	$5.97
Increase in Expensing to $500,000/$2,000,000 and Expansion of Definition of Section 179 Property	2011	Sec. 179(b)(1) and (2) and Sec. 179(f)	P.L. 111-240	h
Reduction in S Corporation Recognition for Built-In Gains Tax	2011	Sec. 1374(d)(7)	P.L. 111-240	$0.07 i
Work Opportunity Tax Credit Targeted to Hiring Qualified Veterans	2012	Sec. 51(c)(4)(B)	P.L. 112-56	na
Additional First-Year Depreciation for 50 Percent of Basis of Qualified Property	2012	Sec. 168(k)(1) and Sec. 168(k)(2)	P.L. 111-312	j
Election to Accelerate AMT Credits in Lieu of Additional First-Year Depreciation	2012	Sec. 168(k)(4)	P.L. 111-312	k
Increase in dollar limitation for expensing to $125,000/$500,000 (indexed)	2012	Sec. 179(b)(1), Sec. 179(b)(2), Sec. 179(c)(2), Sec. 179(d)(1)(A)(ii)	P.L. 111-312	$0.311
Charitable Provisions				
Enhanced Charitable Deduction for Corporate Contributions of Computer Equipment for Educational Purposes	2011	Sec. 170(e)(6)	P.L. 111-312	$0.24
Enhanced Charitable Deduction for Contributions of Food Inventory	2011	Sec. 170(e)(3)(C)	P.L. 111-312	$0.14
Enhanced Charitable Deduction for Contributions of Book Inventory to Public Schools	2011	Sec. 170(e)(3)(D)	P.L. 111-312	$0.06
Tax-Free Distributions from Individual Retirement Accounts for Charitable Purposes	2011	Sec. 408(d)(8)	P.L. 111-312	$0.56
Basis Adjustment to Stock of S Corporations Making Charitable Contributions of Property	2011	Sec. 1367(a)	P.L. 111-312	$0.08
Special Rules for Contributions of Capital Gain Real Property for Conservation Purposes	2011	Sec. 170(b)(1)(E) and Sec. 170(b)(2)(B)	P.L. 111-312	$0.12

Provision	Expiration Year	Internal Revenue Code Section	Most Recent Law Which Extended Provision	10-Year-Cost Estimate for 1-Year Extension (billions)
Energy Provisions				
Suspensions of 100%-of-Net-Income Limitation on Percentage Depletion for Oil and Gas from Marginal Wells	2011	Sec. 613A(c)(6)(H)(ii)	P.L. 111-312	$0.13
Special Rule to Implement Electric Transmission Restructuring	2011	Sec. 451(i)	P.L. 111-312	—
Credit for Construction of Energy Efficient New Homes	2011	Sec. 45L(g)	P.L. 111-312	$0.07
Placed-in-Service Date for Refined Coal Production Facilities	2011	Sec.45(d)(8)	P.L. 111-312	$0.11
Mine Rescue Team Training Credit	2011	Sec. 45N	P.L. 111-312	m
Election to Expense Mine-Safety Equipment	2011	Sec. 179E(a)	P.L. 111-312	—
Credit for Energy Efficient Appliance	2011	Sec. 45M(b)	P.L. 111-312	$0.24
Credit for Nonbusiness Energy Property	2011	Sec. 25C(g)	P.L. 111-312	$0.61
Alternative Fuel Vehicle Refueling Property	2011	Sec. 30C(g)(2)	P.L. 111-312	$0.02
Incentives for Alternative Fuel and Alternative Fuel Mixtures	2011	Sec.6426(d)(5). Sec.6427(e)(6)(C), Sec. 6426(e)(3)	P.L. 111-312	$0.16
Incentives for Biodiesel and Renewable Diesel	2011	Sec. 40A; Sec, 6426(c)(6); and Sec. 6427(e)(6)(B)	P.L. 111-312	$1.11
Incentives for Alcohol Fuels	2011	Sec. 40(e)(1)(A); Secs.40(h)(1) and (h)(2); Sec.6426(b)(6); Sec. 6427(e)(6)(A)	P.L. 111-312	$5.42
Grants for Specified Energy Property in Lieu of Tax Credits	2011	Sec. 48(d) and Sec. 1603 of P.L.111-5	P.L. 111-312	$1.31
Credit for Electric Drive Motorcycles, Thee-Wheeled, and Low- Speed Vehicles	2011	Sec. 30(f)	P.L. 111-5a	na
Conversion Credit for Plug-In Electric Vehicles	2011	Sec. 30B(i)(4)	P.L. 111-5a	n

Table 2. (Continued)

Provision	Expiration Year	Internal Revenue Code Section	Most Recent Law Which Extended Provision	10-Year-Cost Estimate for 1-Year Extension (billions)
Qualified Green Building and Sustainable Design Project Bonds	2012o	Sec. 142(1)(9)	P.L. 110-343	p
Cellulosic Biofuel Producer Credit	2012	Sec, 40(b)(6)(H)	P.L.110-246a	$0.02f
Placed-in-Service Date for Wind Facilities Eligible to Claim the Electricity Production Credit	2012	Sec. 45(d)	P.L. 111-5	q
Credit for Production of Indian Coal	2012	Sec. 45(e)(10)(A)(i)	P.L. 109-58a	na
Election to Claim the Energy Credit in Lieu of the Electricity Production Credit for Wind Facilities	2012	Sec.48(a)(5)	P.L. 111-5	r
Special Depreciation Allowance for Cellulosic Biofuel Plant Property	2012	Sec. 168(l)	P.L. 109-432a	s
Community Assistance Provisions				
Qualified Zone Academy Bonds – Allocation of Bond Limitation	2011	Sec. 54E(c)(1)	P.L. 111-312	$0.13
New Markets Tax Credit	2011	Sec. 45D(f)(1)	P.L. 111-312	$0.86
American Samoa Economic Development Credit	2011	Sec. 119 of P.L. 109-432 as amended by Sec.756 of P.L.111-312	P.L. 111-312	$0.02
Tax Incentives for Investment in the District of Columbia ("DC")	2011	Sec. 1400(f)(1), Sec. 1400A(b), Sec. 1400B(b)(2)(A)(i), Sec. 1400B(b)(3)(A), Sec. 1400B(b)(4)(A)(i), Sec.1400B(b)(4)(B)(i)(I), Sec. 1400B(e)(2) and Sec. 1400B(g)(2)	P.L. 111-312	$0.08

Provision	Expiration Year	Internal Revenue Code Section	Most Recent Law Which Extended Provision	10-Year-Cost Estimate for 1-Year Extension (billions)
Empowerment Zone Tax Incentives	2011	Sec. 1391(d)(1)(A)(i), Sec. 1391(h)(2), Sec. 1202(a)(2), Sec.1394, Sec. 1396, Sec. 1397A, Sec. 1397B	P.L. 111-312	$0.25
Disaster Relief Provisions				
New York Liberty Zone – Tax Exempt Bond Financing	2011	Sec. 1400L(d)(2)(D)	P.L. 111-312	$0.06
Tax-Exempt Bond Financing for the Gulf Opportunity (GO) Zone	2011	Sec. 1400N(a)	P.L. 111-312	$0.14
Low-Income Housing Credit Additional Credit for the GO Zone	2011	Sec. 1400N(c)	P.L. 111-312	$0.19
Placed-in-Service Date for Additional Depreciation for specified GO Zone Extension Property	2011	Sec, 1400N(d)(6)	P.L. 111-312	$0.21
Increase in Rehabilitation Credit for Structures Located in the GO Zone	2011	Sec. 1400N(h)	P.L. 111-312	$0.02
Increase in Rehabilitation Credit for Areas Damaged by the 2008 Midwestern Storms	2011	Sec. 702 of Division C of P.L. 110-343	P.L. 110-343a	t
Tax-Exempt Bond Financing for Areas Damaged by the 2008 Midwestern Storms	2012	Sec. 702 of Division C of P.L. 110-343	P.L. 110-343a	na
Tax-Exempt Bond Financing for Areas Damaged by Hurricane Ike in 2008	2012	Sec. 704 of Division C of P.L. 110-343	P.L. 110-343a	u

Source: Joint Committee on Taxation, List of Expiring Federal Tax Provisions, January 13, 2012, JCX-1-12, Joint Committee on Taxation, Estimated Revenue Effects of an Extensions of Certain Expiring Provisions Through December 31, 2012, December 7, 2011, Table 11-1-167, Department of the Treasury, General Explanation of the Administration's Fiscal Year 2013 Revenue Proposals ("The Greenbook"), February 2012, Table 4, and CRS Report R42105, Tax Provisions Expiring in 2011 and "Tax Extenders", by Molly F. Sherlock, Table 1.

Notes: Accept as otherwise noted, the revenue loss estimates measure 10-year cost over the 2012-2021 budgetary window of extending expiring provisions for approximately one year (from December 15, 2011 to December 31,2012). Except as otherwise noted, the "expiration year" implies the last day of the given year (i.e., 2012 means the provisions expires on December 31, 2012). Generally, these provisions have been enacted and extended more than once. However, this table also includes tax provisions that are expiring that have not previously been extended. For provisions for which a cost estimate of a 1-year extension is not available, recent revenue loss estimates are included in the footnotes, along with the Joint Committee on Taxation (JCT) source. "na" means a revenue loss estimate is not available.

For more information on individual provisions, see U.S. Congress, Senate Committee on the Budget, Tax Expenditures: Compendium of Background Material on Individual Provisions, committee print, prepared by the Congressional Research Service, 111th Cong., 2nd sess., December 2010.

a This law was the first law to enact this provision.

b At enactment, this provision was estimated to result in a revenue gain of less than $1 million over the 2009-2018 budgetary window (JCX-80-08).

c At enactment, this provision was estimated to result in $33 million in revenue losses over the 2008-2018 budgetary window (JCX-64-08).

d A proposed extension of this provision is estimated to result in $430 million in revenue losses over the 2013-2022 budgetary window (FY2013 Greenbook).

e At enactment, this provision was estimated to result in $8 million in revenue losses over the 2011-2020 budgetary window (JCX-54-10).

f This cost estimate reflects the cost over the 2013-2022 budgetary window of extending this provision through the end of 2013. These revenue loss estimates are from Table 4 of the FY2013 Treasury Greenbook.

g A proposed extension of this provision is estimated to result in $4 million in revenue losses over the 2013-2022 budgetary window (FY2013 Greenbook).

h A previous extension of this provision resulted in an estimated $2.18 billion in revenue losses over the 2011-2020 budgetary window (JCX-48-10).

i One-year extension for 2011, with budgetary cost over the 2011-2020 budgetary window (JCX-48-10).

j A previous extension of the combined costs of the increase in first-year depreciation to 100% and extending the 50% additional first-year depreciation for property placed in service after 13/31/2011 of this provision resulted in an estimated $20.88 billion in revenue losses over the 2011-2020 budgetary window (JCX-54-10).

k A previous extension of this provision resulted in an estimates $639 million in revenue losses over the 2011-2020 budgetary window (JCX-54-10).

l One-year extension for 2012, with budgetary cost over the 2011-2020 budgetary window (JCX-54-10).

m A proposed extension of this provision is estimated to result in $2 million in revenue losses over the 2013-2022 budgetary window (FY2013 Greenbook).

n At enactment, the modification of the alternative motor vehicle credit, the credit for qualified plug-in electric drive motor vehicles and the credit for plug-in electric conversion was estimated to result in $2 billion in revenue losses over the 2009-2019 budgetary window (JCX-19-09).

o This provision was scheduled to expire September 30, 2012.

p A previous extension of this provision resulted in an estimated $45 million in revenue losses over the 2009-2018 budgetary window (JCX-78-08).

q A previous extension of this provision for a variety of renewable technologies (i.e., not exclusively wind) resulted in $13.14 billion in revenue losses over the 2009- 2019 budgetary window (JCX-19-09).

r A previous extension of this provision for a variety of renewable technologies (i.e., not exclusively wind) resulted in $285 million in revenue losses over the 2009-2019 budgetary window (JCX-19-09).

s At enactment, this provision was estimated to result in $9 million in revenue losses over the 2007-2016 budgetary window (JCX-51-06).

t At enactment, this provision was estimated to result in $3 million in revenue losses over the 2009-2018 budgetary window (JCX-78-08).

u At enactment, tax exempt bond financing for areas damaged by the 2008 Midwestern storms and low-income housing tax relief for areas damaged by Hurricane Ike was estimated to result in $638 million in revenue losses over the 2009-2019 budgetary window (JCX-78-08).

Congress may instead choose to allow all temporary provisions to expire. According to CBO, this will result in a considerable rise in revenue that will have a significant effect on reducing the projected future deficit.[78] However, some economists warn that the scheduled expiration of these temporary provisions, which would occur simultaneously with the scheduled expiration of emergency unemployment insurance benefits and scheduled budget cuts under the Budget Control Act, would reduce real GDP growth.[79]

Finally, Congress may choose to balance the objectives of deficit reduction and economic assistance by extending certain provisions it determines are effective, while letting others expire. Alternatively, Congress may pursue this objective by considering a fundamental reform of the tax code.[80]

End Notes

[1] This report does not include the budgetary impact of every policy that is scheduled to expire in the next two years. For more information on other policies that are set to expire, see Table 27-6 in the Analytical Perspectives of the President's FY2012 Budget. In addition, for a list of expiring tax provisions, see Joint Committee on Taxation, *List Of Expiring Federal Tax Provisions 2010-2020*, JCX-2-11.

[2] For example, at the end of 2010, Congress enacted the payroll tax cut and extended the Bush tax cuts, the AMT-patch and tax extenders as part of P.L. 111-312. In 2008, Congress extended the AMT patch and certain tax extenders as part of the Emergency Economic Stabilization Act of 2008 (EESA; P.L. 110-343). For other extending legislation, see Table 1 in CRS Report R42105, *Tax Provisions Expiring in 2011 and "Tax Extenders,"* by Molly F. Sherlock.

[3] For example, on March 13, 2012, the Senate considered senate amendment 1812 to S. 1813. Senate amendment 1812 proposed extending certain energy tax extenders. This amendment was not agreed to. In addition, the extension of the payroll tax cut through the end of 2012 was enacted in the 112th Congress.

[4] Other laws enacted during the Bush Administration accelerated the implementation of certain provisions of EGTRRA and JGTRRA or modified provisions in these bills, including the Working Families Tax Relief Act of 2004 (WFTRA; P.L. 108-311), The Tax Increase Prevention and Reconciliation Act of 2005 (TIPRA; P.L. 109-222) and the Emergency Economic Stabilization Act of 2008 (EESA; P.L. 110-343).

[5] For a more detailed analysis of the gradual phase-in of the Bush tax cuts, see CRS Report R41111, *Expiration and Extension of the Individual Income Tax Cuts First Enacted in 2001 and 2003: Background and Analysis*, by James M. Bickley.

[6] For more information, see http://www.irs.gov/pub/irs-drop/rp-11-52.pdf and http://www.tax policycenter.org taxtopics/TCE_CompareRates_2012.cfm.

[7] For more information, see CRS Report R41796, *Deficit Reduction: The Economic and Tax Revenue Effects of Personal Exemption Phaseout (PEP) and Limitation on Itemized Deductions (Pease)*, by Thomas L. Hungerford.

[8] EGTRRA also phased out generation-skipping taxes over a 10-year period, with the gift tax the only federal transfer tax in effect in 2010. For more information on the estate tax, generation-skipping taxes and the gift tax, see CRS Report 95-416, *Federal Estate, Gift, and Generation-Skipping Taxes: A Description of Current Law*, by John R. Luckey.

[9] These exemption amounts are per decedent and a surviving spouse may also use any unused applicable exclusion amount of their spouse.

[10] For more information on this change, see CRS Report RS21352, *The Earned Income Tax Credit (EITC): Changes for 2011 and 2012*, by Christine Scott.

[11] For more information on the American Opportunity Tax Credit, see CRS Report R41967, *Higher Education Tax Benefits: Brief Overview and Budgetary Effects*, by Margot L. Crandall-Hollick and Mark P. Keightley.

[12] Joint Committee on Taxation, *Estimated Budget Effects of the "Tax Relief Unemployment Insurance Reauthorization and Job Creation Act of 2010", Scheduled for Consideration by the United States Senate*, December 10, 2010, JCX-54- 10.

[13] For more information about the budgetary cost of individual provisions in the Bush tax cuts, see Table 1 in CRS Report R42020, *The 2001 and 2003 Bush Tax Cuts and Deficit Reduction*, by Thomas L. Hungerford.

[14] The estate tax is assumed to be extended at the levels under the 2010 Tax Act (P.L. 111-312).

[15] CBO, *The Budget and Economic Outlook: Fiscal Years 2012 to 2022*, January 2012, Table 1-6.

[16] In a later analysis of the budgetary cost of the Bush tax cuts, CBO stated: "The policies [Bush tax cuts] undoubtedly exerted at least some influence on the economy...Those economic feedbacks on today's budget, however, are likely to be modest." For more information, see Congressional Budget Office, *Letter to the Honorable John M. Spratt, Jr.*, July 20, 2007, http://www.cbo.gov/sites/default/files/cbofiles/ftpdocs/83xx/doc8337/07-20-egtrra-jgtrra_and_deficits.pdf.

[17] Lowering marginal tax rates would theoretically increase the amount taxpayers work and so would theoretically increase their income (all else being equal). The sensitivity of income to changes in marginal tax rates is referred to as elasticity. An elasticity less than one implies that changes in taxpayers' income were proportionally less than the changes in the tax rate, while an elasticity greater than one implies that income gains are proportionally larger than the tax cut. A recent review of other studies found that the elasticity of income to tax rate changes was between 0.12 and 0.40. Since the resulting increase in income is proportionally smaller than the cut in marginal rates, government revenues will fall as a result of the cut. See Emmanuel Saez, Joel Slemrod, and Seth Giertz, "The Elasticity of Taxable Income with Respect to Marginal Tax Rates: A Critical Review," *Journal of Economic Literature*, vol. 50, no. 1 (2012), pp. 42. Similarly, CBO found that a 10% tax rate cut would offset between 5% and 32% of the cost of cut in terms of revenue losses over the second 5 years of a year budgetary window. For more information, see Congressional Budget Office, *Analyzing the Economic and Budgetary Effects of a 10 Percent Cut in Income Tax Rates*, Economic and Budget Issue Brief, December 1, 2005, http://www.cbo.gov/sites/default /files /cbofiles/ftpdocs/69xx/doc6908/12-01- 10percenttaxcut.pdf. In so far as tax cuts are deficit-financed, they may actually negatively impact growth. For example, the Joint Committee on Taxation, in modeling the economic effects of reducing individual and corporate tax rates, found that "Growth eventually become(s) negative without offsetting fiscal policy...because accumulating Federal government debt crowds out private investment." Joint Committee on Taxation, *Macroeconomic Analysis of Various Proposals to Provide $500 Billion in Tax Relief*, JCX-4-05, March 1, 2005, p. 2.

[18] For more information, see CRS Report RL32502, *What Effects Did the 2001 to 2003 Tax Cuts Have on the Economy?*, by Marc Labonte.

[19] According to CBO, a 10% cut in income tax rates would result in economic changes that would offset between 1% and 22% of the revenue loss from the tax cut over the first five years." For more information, see Congressional Budget Office, *Analyzing the Economic and Budgetary Effects of a 10 Percent Cut in Income Tax Rates*, Economic and Budget Issue Brief, December 1, 2005, http://www.cbo.gov/sites/default/files/cbofiles /ftpdocs/69xx /doc6908/12-01- 10percenttaxcut.pdf.

[20] William Gale and Peter Orzag, "Bush Administration Tax Policy: Short-Term Stimulus," *Tax Notes*, November 1, 2004, http://www.taxpolicycenter.org/UploadedPDF /1000700_ Tax_Break_11-01-04.pdf.

[21] CBO, Policies for Increasing Economic Growth and Employment in 2012 and 2013, November 2012 and 2013, November 2011, http://www.cbo.gov/publication/42717. Of the policies examined, tax cuts were one of the least stimulative.

[22] Mark Zandi, chief economist at Moody's Analytics, testified to the Joint Economic Committee that the scheduled spending cuts included in the Budget Control Act which go into effect in 2013 and combined expiration of extended unemployment insurance benefits, the payroll tax cuts, and the Bush tax cuts in 2013 will reduce real GDP growth by nearly 3 percentage points in 2013. See http://jec.senate.gov/public//index.cfm?a=Files.Serve&File_id= df8f2728-94fa4339-992a-a9b8d2505fc2.

[23] CBO, *Change in CBO's Baseline Projection of the Surplus Since January 2001*, May 12, 2011, http://www.cbo.gov/ sites/default/files/cbofiles/ftpdocs/121xx/doc12187/changesbaselineprojections.pdf.

[24] The top 20% of taxpayers had an average income of $257,308 in 2010. These estimates include the impact of the AMT-patch and the 2008 EESA recovery payments. See Tax Policy Center. Table T10-0232.

[25] The top 1% of taxpayers had an average income of $1.56 million. Tax Policy Center. These estimates include the impact of the AMT-patch and the 2008 EESA recovery payments. Table T10-0232.

[26] Specifically, 0.6% of the tax cuts accrued to the bottom 20%, 6.1% accrued to next lowest 20% and 10% accrued to the middle 20%. These estimates include the impact of the AMT-patch and the 2008 EESA recovery payments. Table T10-0232.

[27] CBO, *Average Federal Tax Rates in 2007*, June 2010, Table 1, http://www.cbo.gov /sites/default/files/cbofiles/attachments/AverageFedTaxRates2007.pdf.

[28] Tax Policy Center. These estimates include the impact of the AMT-patch and the 2008 EESA recovery payments. Table T10-0232.

[29] For example see, Emmanuel Saez, "Striking It Richer: The Evolution of Top Income in the United States (Updated with 2009 and 2010 estimates)," March 2, 2012, http://emlab.berkeley.edu/~saez/saez-UStopincomes-2010.pdf. In addition, see CRS Report R42400, *The U.S. Income Distribution and Mobility: Trends and International Comparisons*, by Linda Levine.

[30] CBO, *Trends in the Distribution of Household Income Between 1979 and 2007*, October. 2011.

[31] The current federal income tax is progressive meaning that taxes as a share of income increases as income levels of increase.

[32] CBO, *Trends in the Distribution of Household Income Between 1979 and 2007*, October. 2011, p. 20.

[33] CBO, *Trends in the Distribution of Household Income Between 1979 and 2007*, October 2011, p. 27.

[34] See CRS Report R42020, *The 2001 and 2003 Bush Tax Cuts and Deficit Reduction*, by Thomas L. Hungerford.

[35] For more information on the Alternative Minimum Tax, see CRS Report RL30149, *The Alternative Minimum Tax for Individuals*, by Steven Maguire.

[36] For more information, see http://www.taxpolicycenter.org/taxfacts/displayafact.cfm?Docid=195. In addition, see CRS Report RL30149, *The Alternative Minimum Tax for Individuals*, by Steven Maguire.

[37] The last AMT patch which was included in P.L. 111-312 retroactively patched the AMT for 2010 as well as patching it for 2011.

[38] See Table 1 of CRS Report RL30149, *The Alternative Minimum Tax for Individuals*, by Steven Maguire.

[39] These credits include the dependent care credit, the credit for the elderly and disabled, the child credit, the credit for interest on certain home mortgages, the Hope Scholarship and Lifetime Learning credits, the credit for savers, the credit for certain nonbusiness energy property, the credit for residential energy efficient property, the credit for certain plug-in electric vehicles, the credit for alternative motor vehicles, the credit for new qualified plug-in electric drive motor vehicles, and the D.C. first-time homebuyer credit.

[40] These estimates assume that the AMT exemption amount will be raised to $50,650 for unmarried taxpayers and $78,850 for married taxpayers, in addition to extending the allowance of personal credits against the AMT. Joint Committee on Taxation, *Estimated Revenue Effects of an Extensions of Certain Expiring Provisions Through December 31, 2012*, December 7, 2011, Table 11-1-167.

[41] CBO, *The Budget and Economic Outlook: Fiscal Years 2012 to 2022*, January 2012, Table 1-6.

[42] CBO, *The Budget and Economic Outlook: Fiscal Years 2012 to 2022*, January 2012, Table 1-6.

[43] The Tax Policy Center estimates that over 31 million taxpayers will owe the AMT in 2012 without an AMT "patch." For more information, see http://www.taxpolicycenter.org /taxtopics/AMT.cfm.

[44] Some experts have suggested eliminating the regular income tax and simply making the AMT the only income tax. According to certain analysts, it would have been less costly in 2009 to eliminate the regular income tax than the AMT. For more information, see Leonard E. Burman and David Weiner, *Suppose They Took the AM Out of AMT?*, The Urban Institute, Discussion Paper No. 25, August 2005, http://www.taxpolicycenter.org/UploadedPDF/311212_TPC_DiscussionPaper_25.pdf.

[45] For more information on the payroll tax cut, see CRS Report R42103, *Extending the Temporary Payroll Tax Reduction: A Brief Description and Economic Analysis*, by Donald J. Marples and Molly F. Sherlock and CRS Report R41648, *Social Security: Temporary Payroll Tax Reduction*, by Dawn Nuschler.

[46] The payroll tax cut did not reduce employer's share of payroll taxes. The social security payroll tax (prior to the payroll tax reduction) is 12.4%. Statutorily, employer's pay half of the tax (6.2%) and employees pay the other half (6.2%), although many economists believe that workers end up bearing the entire cost of the tax in reduced wages.

[47] The social security tax wage base was $106,800 in 2011. http://www.ssa.gov/oact/COLA /cbb.html.

[48] Under statute, the payroll tax reduction does not reduce funds to the Social Security Trust fund. Funds equal to the loss in payroll tax receipts resulting from the temporary payroll tax reduction are transferred from the general fund to the Social Security trust fund.

[49] Joint Committee on Taxation, JCX-54-10, Joint Committee on Taxation, JCX-57-11, and Joint Committee on Taxation, JCX-17-12.

[50] According to the Social Security Administration, 159 million people will hold jobs subject to the payroll tax. For more information, see http://www.socialsecurity.gov/OACT/FACTS/.

[51] http://www.socialsecurity.gov/OACT/FACTS/.

[52] For more information on analyzing the stimulus impact of a policy, see CRS Report R42103, *Extending the Temporary Payroll Tax Reduction: A Brief Description and Economic Analysis*, by Donald J. Marples and Molly F. Sherlock.

[53] CBO, Policies for Increasing Economic Growth and Employment in 2012 and 2013, November 2011, http://www.cbo.gov/publication/42717, p. 29.

[54] For more information, see Mark Zandi, *Global Policy Prescriptions: How Another Recession Can Be Avoided*, Moody's Analytics, August 26, 2011, p. 6, http://www.economy.com /mark-zandi/documents/Policy-Prescriptions20110826.pdf?src=DS and *"Policy Prescriptions for the Economy,"* Written Testimony of Mark Zandi Before the Senate Budget Committee, September 15, 2011, Table 2, http://www.economy.com/mark-zandi/ documents/FinalSenate-Budget-Committee-091511.pdf.

[55] Some of the provisions expire after 2012. A complete list can be found in Joint Committee on Taxation, *List of Expiring Federal Tax Provisions*, January 13, 2012, JCX-1-12. In addition, for an overview of laws which have extended individual provisions, see Table in CRS Report R42105, *Tax Provisions Expiring in 2011 and "Tax Extenders,"* by Molly F. Sherlock.

[56] For more information, see CRS Report RL32781, *Federal Deductibility of State and Local Taxes*, by Steven Maguire.

[57] For more information, see CRS Report R41967, *Higher Education Tax Benefits: Brief Overview and Budgetary Effects*, by Margot L. Crandall-Hollick and Mark P. Keightley.

[58] For more information, see CRS Report RL33633, *Tax Benefits for Families: Adoption*, by Christine Scott.

[59] For more information, see CRS Report RS21682, The Tax Deduction for Classroom Expenses of Elementary and Secondary School Teachers, by Linda Levine (out of print; available upon request from author).

[60] For more information, see CRS Report RL31181, *Research Tax Credit: Current Law, Legislation in the 112th Congress, and Policy Issues* , by Gary Guenther.

[61] For more information, see CRS Report R41852, *U.S. International Corporate Taxation: Basic Concepts and Policy Issues*, by Mark P. Keightley.

[62] For more information, see CRS Report RL31852, *Section 179 and Bonus Depreciation Expensing Allowances: Current Law, Legislative Proposals in the 112th Congress, and Economic Effects*, by Gary Guenther.

[63] For more information, see CRS Report RL34608, *Tax Issues Relating to Charitable Contributions and Organizations*, by Jane G. Gravelle and Molly F. Sherlock.

[64] For more information, see CRS Report R40110, *Biofuels Incentives: A Summary of Federal Programs*, by Brent D. Yacobucci.

[65] For more information, see CRS Report R41635, *ARRA Section 1603 Grants in Lieu of Tax Credits for Renewable Energy: Overview, Analysis, and Policy Options*, by Phillip Brown and Molly F. Sherlock.

[66] For more information, see CRS Report R42089, *Residential Energy Tax Credits: Overview and Analysis*, by Margot L. Crandall-Hollick and Molly F. Sherlock.

[67] For more information, see CRS Report RL34402, *New Markets Tax Credit: An Introduction*, by Donald J. Marples.

[68] For more information, see CRS Report R41639, *Empowerment Zones, Enterprise Communities, and Renewal Communities: Comparative Overview and Analysis*, by Oscar R. Gonzales and Donald J. Marples.

[69] For more information, see CRS Report RS22344, *The Gulf Opportunity Zone Act of 2005*, by Erika K. Lunder.

[70] Joint Committee on Taxation, *Estimated Revenue Effects of an Extensions of Certain Expiring Provisions Through December 31, 2012*, December 7, 2011, Table 11-1-167.

[71] Department of the Treasury, *General Explanation of the Administration's Fiscal Year 2013 Revenue Proposals ("The Greenbook")*, February 2012, Table 4.

[72] These estimates reflect the impact of extending 80 expiring provisions which expire over the next ten years. Most of the provisions expired at the end of 2011.

[73] CBO, *The Budget and Economic Outlook: Fiscal Years 2012 to 2022*, January 2012, Table 1-6.

[74] For more information, see http://www.taxpolicycenter.org/briefing-book/background/taxes-budget/extenders.cfm.

[75] Senate Committee on Finance, *Hearing on Extenders and Tax reform: Seeking Long-Term Solutions*, Testimony of Dr. Rosanne Altshuler, January 31, 2012, http://finance.senate.gov /hearings/hearing/?id=b1604e2e-5056-a032-52ffdd661f9280f6.

[76] For example, Senator Max Baucus, chairman of the Senate Finance Committee has stated that "Many construction projects, for example, take at least five years to plan, finance and build. When Congress passes an investment tax credit for only one year, there's no guarantee for a town, city or developer to move forward with a five-year project." http://finance.senate.gov/imo/media/doc/01312012_Baucus_Says_Tax_Rules_Should_Help _Businesses_with_LongTerm_Plans_Grow,_Not_Hinder_Them[1]1.pdf. In addition, Senator Hatch, ranking member of the Senate Finance Committee has said that "Even those extenders that are sound tax policy lose much of their power due to their temporary character." http://finance.senate.gov/newsroom/ranking/release/?id=4042ffa9-9861-431a-8ea8- 9e6dc4af513e.

[77] A budget deficit can be "sustainable" if deficits are small enough so that the accumulation of annual deficits—the debt—does not grow faster than GDP. Experts differ on what is the exact size of a sustainable budget deficit, but they generally cite figures below 3% of GDP. Prior CRS analysis estimated that annual budget deficits would need to be no larger than 2.5% to 3.0% of GDP over the next 10 years in order to stabilize the debt as a share of GDP at its projected 2011 level (69% of GDP). For more information, see CRS Report R41778, *Reducing the Budget Deficit: Policy Issues*, by Marc Labonte.

[78] CBO, *The Budget and Economic Outlook: Fiscal Years 2012 to 2022*, January 2012, p. xi.

[79] See Joint Economic Committee, "*Bolstering the Economy: Helping American Families by Reauthorizing the Payroll Tax Cut and UI Benefits*," written Testimony of Mark Zandi, Chief Economist and Co-Founder, Moody's Analytics, February 7, 2012, http://jec.senate.gov/public//index.cfm?a=Files.Serve&File_id=df8f2728-94fa-4339-992a-a9b8d2505fc2.

[80] For more information, see CRS Report R41641, *Reducing the Budget Deficit: Tax Policy Options*, by Molly F. Sherlock and CRS Report R42435, *The Challenge of Individual Income Tax Reform: An Economic Analysis of Tax Base Broadening*, by Jane G. Gravelle and Thomas L. Hungerford.

In: Expiring Federal Tax Provisions: 2012-2022 ISBN: 978-1-62257-123-9
Editors: P. L. Collins and F. R. Peterson

Chapter 2

LIST OF EXPIRING FEDERAL TAX ROVISIONS: 2011-2022*

Joint Committee on Taxation

INTRODUCTION

This document,[1] prepared by the staff of the Joint Committee on Taxation, provides a listing of Federal tax provisions (other than those providing time-limited transition relief after the repeal of an underlying rule) that are currently scheduled to expire in 2011-2022 (with references to the applicable section of the Internal Revenue Code of 1986 or other applicable law).

Expiring Federal tax provisions providing temporary disaster relief are separately listed in Part II of the document.

For purposes of compiling this list, the staff of the Joint Committee on Taxation considers a provision to be expiring if, at a statutorily specified date, the provision expires completely or reverts to the law in effect before the present-law version of the provision. Certain provisions terminate on dates that refer to a taxpayer's taxable year and not a calendar year. For these provisions, the expiration dates listed in this document apply with respect to calendar year taxpayers. The expiration dates of such provisions may differ, however, with

---

* This is an edited, reformatted and augmented version of Joint Committee on Taxation, dated January 6, 2012.

respect to fiscal year taxpayers or taxpayers with short taxable years. Years in which there are no expiring provisions are not listed in the document.

I. Federal Tax Provisions[2] Expiring 2011-2022

A. Provisions Expiring in 2011

Provision (Code section)		Expiration Date
1.	First-time homebuyer credit for individuals on qualified official extended duty outside the United States (sec. 36(h)(3))	4/30/11[3]
2.	Federal Unemployment Tax Act ("FUTA") surtax of 0.2 percent (sec. 3301(1))	6/30/11
3.	Credit for certain nonbusiness energy property (sec. 25C(g))	12/31/11
4.	Personal tax credits allowed against regular tax and alternative minimum tax ("AMT") (sec. 26(a)(2))	12/31/11
5.	Credit for electric drive motorcycles, three-wheeled vehicles, and low-speed vehicles (sec. 30(f))	12/31/11
6.	Conversion credit for plug-in electric vehicles (sec. 30B(i)(4))	12/31/11
7.	Alternative fuel vehicle refueling property (non-hydrogen refueling property) (sec. 30C(g)(2))	12/31/11[4]
8.	Expansion of adoption credit and adoption assistance programs (secs. 36C and 137 and sec. 10909(c) of Pub. L. No. 111-148 as amended by section 101(b) of Pub. L. No. 111-312)	12/31/11
9.	Incentives for alcohol fuels	12/31/11
a.	Alcohol fuels income tax credit (alcohol fuel, alcohol used to produce a qualified mixture, and small ethanol producers) (secs. 40(e)(1)(A), (h)(1), and (h)(2))	
b.	Alcohol fuel mixture excise tax credit and outlay payments (secs. 6426(b)(6) and 6427(e)(6)(A))	12/31/11
10.	Incentives for biodiesel and renewable diesel:	
a.	Income tax credits for biodiesel fuel, biodiesel used to produce a qualified mixture, and small agri-biodiesel producers (sec. 40A)	12/31/11
b.	Income tax credits for renewable diesel fuel and renewable diesel used to produce a qualified mixture (sec. 40A)	12/31/11
c.	Excise tax credits and outlay payments for biodiesel fuel mixtures (secs. 6426(c)(6) and 6427(e)(6)(B))	12/31/11

Provision (Code section)		Expiration Date
d.	Excise tax credits and outlay payments for renewable diesel fuel mixtures (secs. 6426(c)(6) and 6427(e)(6)(B))	12/31/11
11.	Tax credit for research and experimentation expenses (sec. 41(h)(1)(B))	12/31/11
12.	Placed-in-service date for facilities eligible to claim the refined coal production credit (other than refined coal facilities that produce steel industry fuel) (sec. 45(d)(8))	12/31/11
13.	Indian employment tax credit (sec. 45A(f))	12/31/11
14.	New markets tax credit (sec. 45D(f)(1))	12/31/11
15.	Credit for certain expenditures for maintaining railroad tracks (sec. 45G(f))	12/31/11
16.	Credit for construction of new energy efficient homes (sec. 45L(g))	12/31/11
17.	Credit for energy efficient appliances (sec. 45M(b))	12/31/11
18.	Mine rescue team training credit (sec. 45N)	12/31/11
19.	Employer wage credit for activated military reservists (sec. 45P)	12/31/11
20.	Grants for specified energy property in lieu of tax credits (sec. 48(d) and sec. 1603 of Pub. L. No. 111-5)	12/31/11
21.	Work opportunity tax credit (sec. 51(c)(4))	12/31/11[5]
22.	Qualified zone academy bonds: allocation of bond limitation (sec. 54E(c)(1))	12/31/11
23.	Increased AMT exemption amount (sec. 55(d)(1))	12/31/11
24.	Deduction for certain expenses of elementary and secondary school teachers (sec. 62(a)(2)(D))	12/31/11
25.	Parity for exclusion from income for employer-provided mass transit and parking benefits (sec. 132(f))	12/31/11
26.	Treatment of military basic housing allowances under low-income housing credit (sec. 142(d))	12/31/11
27.	Premiums for mortgage insurance deductible as interest that is qualified residence interest (sec. 163(h)(3))	12/31/11
28.	Deduction for State and local general sales taxes (sec. 164(b)(5))	12/31/11

(Continued)

Provision (Code section)		Expiration Date
29.	15-year straight-line cost recovery for qualified leasehold improvements, qualified restaurant buildings and improvements, and qualified retail improvements (secs. 168(e)(3)(E)(iv), (v), (ix), 168(e)(7)(A)(i) and (e)(8))	12/31/11
30.	Seven-year recovery period for motorsports entertainment complexes (sec. 168(i)(15) and 168(e)(3)(C)(ii))	12/31/11
31.	Accelerated depreciation for business property on an Indian reservation (sec. 168(j)(8))	12/31/11
32.	Additional first-year depreciation for 100 percent of basis of qualified property (sec. 168(k)(5))	12/31/116
33.	Special rules for contributions of capital gain real property made for conservation purposes (secs. 170(b)(1)(E) and 170(b)(2)(B))	12/31/11
34.	Enhanced charitable deduction for contributions of food inventory (sec. 170(e)(3)(C))	12/31/11
35.	Enhanced charitable deduction for contributions of book inventories to public schools (sec. 170(e)(3)(D))	12/31/11
36.	Enhanced charitable deduction for corporate contributions of computer equipment for educational purposes (sec. 170(e)(6))	12/31/11
37.	Increase in expensing to $500,000/$2,000,000 and expansion of definition of section 179 property (secs. 179(b)(1) and (2) and 179(f))	12/31/117
38.	Election to expense advanced mine safety equipment (sec. 179E(a))	12/31/11
39.	Special expensing rules for certain film and television productions (sec. 181(f))	12/31/11
40.	Expensing of "brownfields" environmental remediation costs (sec. 198(h))	12/31/11
41.	Deduction allowable with respect to income attributable to domestic production activities in Puerto Rico (sec. 199(d)(8))	12/31/11
42.	Above-the-line deduction for qualified tuition and related expenses (sec. 222(e))	12/31/11
43.	Tax-free distributions from individual retirement plans for charitable purposes (sec. 408(d)(8))	12/31/11
44.	Special rule for sales or dispositions to implement Federal Energy Regulatory Commission ("FERC") or State electric restructuring policy (sec. 451(i))	12/31/11

Provision (Code section)		Expiration Date
45.	Modification of tax treatment of certain payments to controlling exempt organizations (sec. 512(b)(13)(E))	12/31/11
46.	Suspension of 100 percent-of-net-income limitation on percentage depletion for oil and gas from marginal wells (sec. 613A(c)(6)(H)(ii))	12/31/11
47.	Treatment of certain dividends of regulated investment companies ("RICs") (secs. 871(k)(1)(C) and (2)(C), and 881(e)(1)(A) and (2))	12/31/11
48.	RIC qualified investment entity treatment under the Foreign Investment in Real Property Tax Act ("FIRPTA") (sec. 897(h)(4))	12/31/11
49.	Exceptions under subpart F for active financing income (secs. 953(e)(10) and 954(h)(9))	12/31/11
50.	Look-through treatment of payments between related controlled foreign corporations under the foreign personal holding company rules (sec. 954(c)(6))	12/31/11
51.	Special rules for qualified small business stock (sec. 1202(a)(4))	12/31/11
52.	Basis adjustment to stock of S corporations making charitable contributions of property (sec. 1367(a))	12/31/11
53.	Reduction in S corporation recognition period for built-in gains tax (sec. 1374(d)(7))	12/31/11
54.	Empowerment zone tax incentives:8	
a.	Designation of an empowerment zone and of additional empowerment zones (secs. 1391(d)(1)(A)(i) and (h)(2))	12/31/11
b.	Increased exclusion of gain (attributable to periods through 12/31/16) on the sale of qualified business stock of an empowerment zone business (secs. 1202(a)(2) and 1391(d)(1)(A)(i))	12/31/11
c.	Empowerment zone tax-exempt bonds (secs. 1394 and 1391(d)(1)(A)(i))	12/31/11
d.	Empowerment zone employment credit (secs. 1396 and 1391(d)(1)(A)(i))	12/31/11
e.	Increased expensing under sec. 179 (secs. 1397A and 1391(d)(1)(A)(i))	12/31/11
f.	Nonrecognition of gain on rollover of empowerment zone investments (secs. 1397B and 1391(d)(1)(A)(i))	12/31/11
55.	Tax incentives for investment in the District of Columbia ("DC"):	
a.	Designation of DC Zone, employment tax credit, and additional expensing (sec. 1400(f)(1))	12/31/11
b.	DC Zone tax-exempt bonds (sec. 1400A(b))	12/31/11

(Continued)

Provision (Code section)		Expiration Date
c.	Acquisition date for eligibility for zero percent capital gains rate for investment in DC for gains through 12/31/16 (secs. 1400B(b)(2)(A)(i), (b)(3)(A), (b)(4)(A)(i), (b)(4)(B)(i)(I), (e)(2), and (g)(2))	12/31/11
d.	Tax credit for first-time DC homebuyers (sec. 1400C(i))	12/31/11
56.	Definition of gross estate for RIC stock owned by a nonresident not a citizen of the United States (sec. 2105(d))	12/31/11
57.	Disclosure of prisoner return information to certain prison officials (sec. 6103(k)(10))	12/31/11
58.	Incentives for alternative fuel and alternative fuel mixtures (other than liquefied hydrogen):9	
a.	Excise tax credits and outlay payments for alternative fuel (secs. 6426(d)(5) and 6427(e)(6)(C))	12/31/11
b.	Excise tax credits and outlay payments for alternative fuel mixtures (secs. 6426(e)(3) and 6427(e)(6)(C))	12/31/11
59.	Temporary increase in limit on cover over of rum excise tax revenues (from $10.50 to $13.25 per proof gallon) to Puerto Rico and the Virgin Islands (sec. 7652(f))	12/31/11
60.	American Samoa economic development credit (sec. 119 of Pub. L. No. 109-432 as amended by sec. 756 of Pub. L. No. 111-312)	12/31/11

B. Provisions Expiring in 2012

Provision (Code section)		Expiration Date
1.	Airport and Airway Trust Fund excise taxes:	
a.	All but 4.3 cents-per-gallon of taxes on noncommercial aviation kerosene and noncommercial aviation gasoline (sec. 4081(d)(2)(B))	1/31/1210
b.	Domestic and international air passenger ticket taxes (sec. 4261(j)(1)(A)(ii))	1/31/12
c.	Air cargo tax (sec. 4271(d)(1)(A)(ii))	1/31/12
2.	Temporary payroll tax cut (sec. 101 of Pub. L. No. 112-78)	2/29/12
3.	Highway Trust Fund excise tax rates:	

Provision (Code section)		Expiration Date
a.	All but 4.3 cents-per-gallon of the taxes on highway gasoline, diesel fuel, kerosene, and alternative fuels (secs. 4041(a) and 4081(d)(1))	3/31/1211
b.	Reduced rate of tax on partially exempt methanol or ethanol fuel (sec. 4041(m))	3/31/1212
c.	Tax on retail sale of heavy highway vehicles (sec. 4051(c))	3/31/12
d.	Tax on heavy truck tires (sec. 4071(d))	3/31/12
e.	Annual use tax on heavy highway vehicles (sec. 4481(f))	9/30/12
4.	Leaking Underground Storage Tank Trust Fund financing rate (secs. 4041(d)(4) and 4081(d)(3))	3/31/12
5.	Qualified green buildings and sustainable design project bonds (sec. 142(l)(8))	9/30/12
6.	Increase of the size of 15 percent rate bracket for married filers to double that of unmarried filers (sec. 1(f)(8) and sec. 901 of Pub. L. No. 107-16)	12/31/12
7.	Reduced capital gain rates for individuals (secs. 1(h), 55(b), 57(a)(7), 1445(e)(1), 7518(g)(6)(A) and sec. 303 of Pub. L. No. 108-27)	12/31/12
8.	Dividends of individuals taxed at capital gain rates (secs. 1(h)(11), 163(d)(4)(B), 854(a) and (b), and 857(c) and sec. 303 of Pub. L. No. 108-27)	12/31/12
9.	Ten percent individual income tax rate (sec. 1(i) and sec. 901 of Pub. L. No. 107-16)	12/31/12
10.	Reduction in other individual income tax rates: size of 15 percent rate bracket modified to reflect 10 percent rate, and 28 percent, 31 percent, 36 percent, and 39.6 percent rates are reduced to 25 percent, 28 percent, 33 percent, and 35 percent, respectively (sec. 1(i)(2) and sec. 901 of Pub. L. No. 107-16)	12/31/12
11.	Dependent care credit: increase of dollar limit on creditable expenses from $2,400 to $3,000 ($4,800 to $6,000 for two or more children), increase of applicable credit percentage from 30 to 35 percent, increase of beginning point of phase-out range from $10,000 to $15,000 (secs. 21(a)(2) and 21(c) and sec. 901 of Pub. L. No. 107-16)	12/31/12
12.	Adoption credit and adoption assistance exclusion: increase to $10,000 for maximum credit and maximum exclusion, special needs adoptions deemed to have $10,000 eligible expenses for purposes of credit and exclusion, increase the beginning and ending points of phase-out range for credit and exclusion, allow the credit against AMT (secs. 23 and 137 and sec. 901 of Pub. L. No. 107-16)	12/31/12

(Continued)

Provision (Code section)		Expiration Date
13.	Child credit: increase from $500 to $1,000, expand eligibility for refundable portion of the credit, AMT relief, provide that child credit not treated as income or resources for purposes of benefit or assistance programs financed in whole or in part with Federal funds (secs. 24(a), (b)(3), and (d) and secs. 203 and 901 of Pub. L. No. 107-16)	12/31/12
14.	American opportunity tax credit (sec. 25A(i))	12/31/12
15.	Earned income tax credit ("EITC"): increase in the beginning point of the phase-out range for joint returns, modification of EITC treatment of amounts not includible in income, repeal of reduction of EITC for AMT liability, expansion of math error authority (secs. 32(b)(2), (c)(2)(A)(i), (h), and 6213(g)(2) and sec. 901 of Pub. L. No. 107-16)	12/31/12
16.	Earned income tax credit:	
a.	Credit percentage of 45 percent for three or more qualifying children (sec. 32(b)(3)(A))	12/31/12
b.	Phaseout threshold for marriage penalty relief (sec. 32(b)(3)(B))	12/31/12
17.	Cellulosic biofuel producer credit (sec. 40(b)(6)(H))	12/31/12
18.	Placed-in-service date for wind facilities eligible to claim electricity production credit (sec. 45(d))	12/31/12
19.	Credit for production of Indian coal (sec. 45(e)(10)(A)(i))	12/31/12
20.	Credit for employer-provided child care (sec. 45F and sec. 901 of Pub. L. No. 107-16)	12/31/12
21.	Election to claim the energy credit in lieu of the electricity production credit for wind facilities (sec. 48(a)(5))	12/31/12
22.	Work opportunity tax credit targeted to hiring qualified veterans (sec. 51(c)(4)(B))	12/31/12
23.	Credit for prior year minimum tax liability made refundable after period of years (sec. 53(e))	12/31/12
24.	Increase of the standard deduction for married filers to double that of unmarried filers (sec. 63(c)(2)(A) and sec. 901 of Pub. L. No. 107-16)	12/31/12
25.	Repeal of overall limitation on itemized deductions (the "Pease limitation") (sec. 68(g) and sec. 901 of Pub. L. No. 107-16)	12/31/12
26.	Discharge of indebtedness on principal residence excluded from gross income of individuals (sec. 108(a)(1)(E))	12/31/12
27.	Elimination of tax on awards under the National Health Service Corps Scholarship Program and the F. Edward Hébert Armed Forces Health Professions Scholarship and Financial Assistance Program (sec. 117(c)(2) and sec. 901 of Pub. L. No. 107-16)	12/31/12

Provision (Code section)		Expiration Date
28.	Employer-provided educational assistance: expansion to graduate education and making the exclusion permanent (sec. 127(c)(1) and sec. 901 of Pub. L. No. 107-16)	12/31/12
29.	Tax-exempt bonds for educational facilities: increase in amount of bonds qualifying for small-issuer arbitrage rebate exception, expansion of tax-exempt bond treatment to public school facilities (secs. 142(a)(13) and (k), 148(f)(4)(D)(vii) and sec. 901 of Pub. L. No. 107-16)	12/31/12
30.	Repeal of the personal exemptions phase-outs ("PEP") for high-income taxpayers (sec. 151(d)(3)(F) and sec. 901 of Pub. L. No. 107-16)	12/31/12
31.	Additional first-year depreciation for 50 percent of basis of qualified property (secs. 168(k)(1) and (2))	12/31/12
32.	Election to accelerate AMT credits in lieu of additional first-year depreciation (sec. 168(k)(4))	12/31/12
33.	Special depreciation allowance for cellulosic biofuel plant property (sec. 168(l))	12/31/12
34.	Increase in dollar limitations for expensing to $125,000/500,000 (indexed) (secs. 179(b)(1) and (2), (c)(2), and (d)(1)(A)(ii))	12/31/12
35.	Student loan interest deduction: increase and indexation for inflation of the phase-out ranges, repeal of the limit on the number of months that interest payments are deductible, repeal of the rule that voluntary payments of interest are not deductible (sec. 221 and sec. 901 of Pub. L. No. 107-16)	12/31/12
36.	Repeal of collapsible corporation rules (sec. 341 and sec. 303 of Pub. L. No. 108-27)	12/31/12
37.	Education Individual Retirement Accounts (Coverdell education savings accounts): increase of maximum annual contribution from $500 to $2,000, expansion of definition of qualified education expenses, increase in the size of the phase-out range for married filers to double that of unmarried filers, provision of special needs beneficiary rules, contributions by corporations and other entities, and contributions until April 15th, permitted (secs. 530(b)(1), (b)(2), (b)(4), (c)(1), (d)(2) and sec. 901 of Pub. L. No. 107-16)	12/31/12
38.	Reduced rates under accumulated earnings tax and personal holding company tax (secs. 531 and 541 and sec. 901 of Pub. L. No. 107-16)	12/31/12
39.	Modified tax treatment of electing Alaska Native Settlement Trusts and their beneficiaries (sec. 646 and sec. 901 of Pub. L. No. 107-16)	12/31/12
40.	Estate, gift, and generation skipping transfer tax provisions (sec. 901 of Pub. L. No. 107-16):	

(Continued)

Provision (Code section)		Expiration Date
a.	Reduction in the maximum estate and gift tax rate to 35 percent (secs. 2001 and 2502)	12/31/12
b.	Modifications of estate and gift taxes to reflect differences in credit resulting from different tax rates (secs. 2001(b)(2), 2001(g), and 2505(a))	12/31/12
c.	Increase in estate and gift tax exemption to $5 million (indexed for inflation in years after 2011) (sec. 2010)	12/31/12
d.	"Portability" rules permitting a surviving spouse to use the deceased spousal unused exclusion amount (sec. 2010(c))	12/31/12
e.	Estate tax deduction for State death taxes paid (secs. 2011, 2053, 2058, 2102, 2106, and 2604)	12/31/12
f.	Expansion and clarification of estate tax conservation easement rules (secs. 2031(c)(2) and (c)(8)(A)(i))	12/31/12
g.	Repeal of the qualified family-owned business deduction (sec. 2057)	12/31/12
h.	Modifications to generation-skipping transfer tax rules regarding deemed allocations of exemption to certain transfers in trust, severing of trusts, valuation, and relief for late elections (secs. 2632(c) and 2642(a)(3), (b)(1), and (b)(2)(A))	12/31/12
i.	Modifications to estate tax installment payment rules (secs. 6166(b)(1)(B)(ii), (b)(1)(C)(ii), (b)(8)(B), (b)(9)(B)(iii)(I), and (b)(10))	12/31/12
41.	Refunds disregarded in the administration of Federal programs and Federally assisted programs (sec. 6409)	12/31/12

C. Provisions Expiring in 2013

Provision (Code section)		Expiration Date
1.	Credit for health insurance costs of eligible individuals (sec. 35(a))	12/31/13
2.	Determination of low-income housing credit rate (sec. 42(b)(2))	12/31/13
3.	Placed-in-service date for facilities (other than wind facilities) eligible to claim the electricity production credit (sec. 45(d))	12/31/1323
4.	Election to claim the energy credit in lieu of the electricity production credit for renewable power facilities other than wind facilities (sec. 48(a)(5))	12/31/1324

Provision (Code section)		Expiration Date
5.	Three-year depreciation for race horses two years old or younger (sec. 168(e)(3)(A))	12/31/13
6.	Placed-in-service date for partial expensing of certain refinery property (sec. 179C(c)(1))	12/31/13[25]
7.	Energy efficient commercial buildings deduction (sec. 179D(h))	12/31/13
8.	Transfer of excess pension assets to retiree health accounts (sec. 420(b)(5))	12/31/13

D. Provisions Expiring in 2014

Provision (Code section)		Expiration Date
1.	Incentives for alternative fuel and alternative fuel mixtures involving liquefied hydrogen:	
a.	Excise tax credits and outlay payments for liquefied hydrogen (secs. 6426(d)(5) and 6427(e)(6)(D))	9/30/14[26]
b.	Excise tax credits and outlay payments for liquefied hydrogen fuel mixtures (secs. 6426(e)(3) and 6427(e)(6)(D))	9/30/14
2.	Alternative motor vehicle credit for qualified fuel cell motor vehicles (sec. 30B(k)(1))	12/31/14
3.	Alternative fuel vehicle refueling property (hydrogen refueling property) (sec. 30C(g)(1))	12/31/14[27]
4.	Automatic amortization extension for multiemployer defined benefit pension plans (sec. 431(d)(1)(C))	12/31/14[28]
5.	Additional funding rules for multiemployer defined benefit pension plans in endangered or critical status (sec. 432 and sec. 221(c) of Pub. L. No. 109-280)	12/31/14[29]
6.	Deemed approval of adoption, use or cessation of shortfall funding method for multiemployer defined benefit pension plans (secs. 201(b) and 221(c) of Pub. L. No. 109-280)	12/31/14

E. Provisions Expiring in 2016

Provision (Code section)		Expiration Date
1.	Credit for residential energy property (sec. 25D(g))	12/31/16
2.	Increased credit for business solar energy property (sec. 48(a)(2)(A)(i)(II))	12/31/16
3.	Credit for hybrid solar lighting systems (sec. 48(a)(3)(A)(ii))	12/31/16
4.	Energy credit for geothermal heat pump property, small wind property, and combined heat and power property (secs. 48(a)(3)(A)(vii), 48(c)(4), and 48(c)(3)(A)(iv))	12/31/16
5.	Credit for business installation of qualified fuel cells and stationary microturbine power plants (secs. 48(c)(1)(D) and (c)(2)(D))	12/31/16

F. Provisions Expiring in 2017

	Provision (Code section)	Expiration Date
1.	Oil Spill Liability Trust Fund financing rate (sec. 4611(f)(2))	12/31/17

G. Provisions Expiring in 2018

Provision (Code section)		Expiration Date
1.	Black Lung Disability Trust Fund: increase in amount of excise tax on coal (sec. 4121(e)(2))	12/31/18[30]

H. Provisions Expiring in 2020

Provision (Code section)		Expiration Date
1.	Placed-in-service date for eligibility for the credit for production from certified advanced nuclear power facilities (sec. 45J(d)(1)(B))	12/31/20

II. Temporary Disaster Relief Federal Tax Provisions Expiring 2011-2022

A. Temporary Disaster Relief Federal Tax Provisions Expiring in 2011

Provision (Code section)		Expiration Date
1.	New York Liberty Zone: tax-exempt bond financing (sec. 1400L(d)(2)(D))	12/31/11
2.	Tax-exempt bond financing for the Gulf Opportunity Zone (sec. 1400N(a))	12/31/11
3.	Low-income housing credit additional housing credit dollar amount for the Gulf Opportunity Zone and certain programmatic expansions for the Gulf Opportunity Zone, the Rita GO Zone, and the Wilma GO Zone (sec. 1400N(c))	12/31/11
4.	Placed-in-service date for additional depreciation for specified Gulf Opportunity Zone extension property (sec. 1400N(d)(6))	12/31/11[31]
5.	Increase in rehabilitation credit for structures located in the Gulf Opportunity Zone (sec. 1400N(h))	12/31/11
6.	Increase in rehabilitation credit for areas damaged by 2008 Midwestern severe storms, tornados, and flooding (sec. 702 of Division C of Pub. L. No. 110-343)	12/31/11

B. Temporary Disaster Relief Federal Tax Provisions Expiring in 2012

Provision (Code section)		Expiration Date
1.	Tax-exempt bond financing rules for areas damaged by 2008 Midwestern severe storms, tornados, and flooding (sec. 702 of Division C of Pub. L. No. 110-343)	12/31/12
2.	Tax-exempt bond financing rules for areas damaged by Hurricane Ike in 2008 (sec. 704 of Division C of Pub. L. No. 110-343)	12/31/12

C. Temporary Disaster Relief Federal Tax Provisions Expiring in 2013

Provision (Code section)		Expiration Date
1.	Extension of replacement period for nonrecognition of gain for areas damaged by 2008 Midwestern severe storms, tornados and flooding (sec. 702 of Division C of Pub. L. No. 110-343)	12/31/13

End Notes

[1] This document may be cited as follows: Joint Committee on Taxation, *List of Expiring Federal Tax Provisions 2011-2022* (JCX-1-12), January 6, 2012. This document can be found on the Joint Committee on Taxation website at www.jct.gov.

[2] Not including temporary disaster relief Federal tax provisions, which are listed in Part II.

[3] In the case of a written binding contract entered into before May 1, 2011, to close on the purchase of a principal residence before July 1, 2011, the purchase must close before July 1, 2011.

[4] The related provision of section 30C for hydrogen refueling property expires December 31, 2014.

[5] The work opportunity tax credit targeted to hiring qualified veterans expires December 31, 2012.

[6] December 31, 2012, for certain longer-lived and transportation property. The 50 percent additional first year depreciation deduction (which is effective after December 31, 2011) expires December 31, 2012 (December 31, 2013 for certain longer-lived and transportation property).

[7] The expensing limits of $125,000/$500,000 effective after December 31, 2011 expire December 31, 2012.

[8] The empowerment zone tax incentives may expire earlier than December 31, 2011 if a State or local government provided for an expiration date in the nomination of an empowerment zone, or the appropriate Secretary revokes an empowerment zone's designation. The State or local government may, however, amend the nomination to provide for a new termination date.

[9] The related provisions for liquefied hydrogen fuel expire September 30, 2014.

[10] The 4.3-cents-per-gallon rate is permanent.

[11] The 4.3-cents-per-gallon rate is permanent.

[12] After March 31, 2012, in the case of fuel none of the alcohol in which consists of ethanol, the rate is 2.15 cents-per-gallon. In any other case, the rate is 4.3 cents-per-gallon.

[13] A termination rule applies to all provisions (not otherwise extended or made permanent) that were enacted in EGTRRA (Pub. L. No. 107-16). These provisions terminate December 31, 2012, under EGTRRA section 901 as modified by TRUIRJCA (Pub. L. No. 111-312), and are listed in this document with a reference to section 901 of Pub. L. No. 107-16.

[14] A termination rule applies to provisions relating to (1) reduced capital gains rates, (2) dividends taxed at capital gains rates, and (3) repeal of the collapsible corporation rules, enacted in the Jobs and Growth Tax Relief Reconciliation Act of 2003, Pub. L. No. 108-27 ("JGTRRA"). These provisions terminate December 31, 2012, under JGTRRA section 303 as modified by section 102 of the Tax Increase Prevention and Reconciliation Act of 2005, Pub. L. No. 109-222 ("TIPRA") and section 102 of TRUIRJCA, Pub. L. No. 111-312.

[15] See note 14.

[16] The placed-in-service date for renewable power facilities other than wind facilities is December 31, 2013.

[17] The expiration date with respect to renewable power facilities other than wind facilities is December 31, 2013.

[18] The work opportunity tax credit generally expired December 31, 2011.

[19] December 31, 2013 for certain longer-lived and transportation property.

[20] December 31, 2013 for certain longer-lived and transportation property.

[21] The dollar limitations for expensing at $500,000/$2,000,000 and the expanded definition of section 179 property expire for any taxable year beginning after December 31, 2011.

[22] See note 14.

[23] The placed-in-service date for wind facilities is December 31, 2012.

[24] The expiration date with respect to wind facilities is December 31, 2012.

[25] The commencement-of-construction date for self-constructed property is December 31, 2009.

[26] Related provisions for non-hydrogen fuel expired December 31, 2011.

[27] The related provision of section 30C for non-hydrogen alternative fuel vehicle refueling property expired December 31, 2011.

[28] A corresponding provision, also expiring on December 31, 2014, is contained in section 304(d)(1)(C) of ERISA.

[29] A corresponding provision, also expiring on December 31, 2014, is contained in section 305 of ERISA.

[30] The increased amount of the excise tax on coal terminates the earlier of this date or the first December 31 as of which there is no balance of repayable advances made to the Black Lung Disability Trust Fund and no unpaid interest on such advances.

[31] Certain personal property may qualify if placed in service within 90 days following December 31, 2011.

INDEX